I WAS DOCTOR
MENGELE'S ASSISTANT

Miklós Nyiszli 1901–1956

MIKLÓS NYISZLI

I WAS DOCTOR
MENGELE'S ASSISTANT

THE MEMOIRS OF AN AUSCHWITZ PHYSICIAN

Translated from Polish by
Witold Zbirohowski-Kościa

OŚWIĘCIM 2001

Original Hungarian title:
Orvos voltam Auschwitzban

Polish edition:
Byłem asystentem doktora Mengele, Oświęcim 2000

Editing and footnotes:
Franciszek Piper

Consultation:
Marta Szesztay (Hungary)

Photographs and documents:
Auschwitz-Birkenau State Museum at Oświęcim

ISBN 83-906992-7-3

Distribution: *Frap-Books*
e-mail: frapb@poczta.onet.pl

Typesetting: *Oficyna Wydawnicza „Impuls"*
Printed in Poland by Poligrafia Inspektoratu Towarzystwa
Salezjańskiego, ul. Konfederacka 6, 30-306 Kraków

TESTIMONY

I, the undersigned, Dr Miklós Nyiszli[1], physician and former prisoner of Auschwitz concentration camp No A-8450, testify that as an eyewitness employed at the Birkenau crematoria and pyres that devoured millions of fathers, mothers and children have written my account of this, the darkest chapter of human history, according to the truth, objectively, without any exaggeration or embellishment[2].

As a doctor at the crematoria of Auschwitz, I have had to draft and sign with the number tattooed on my own arm innumerable medical and forensic reports regarding post-mortems. These documents were countersigned by my SS supervisor, Mengele[3], and then sent by post to: *Berlin-Dahlem, Institut für Rassenbiologische und Antropologishe Forschungen*[4], the address of one of the most renowned medical establishments in the world. In all probability these documents can still be found in the archives of this great institute. The object of my account is not literary success. I am a doctor, not a writer.

Nagyvárad, March 1946

Miklós Nyiszli MD

I

A hot May afternoon. The stench from the brimming buckets and the ninety unwashed, sweating bodies, crammed together inside a freight car with only one tiny barbed-wired window, was becoming increasingly unbearable. The train of deportees was made up of forty such boxcars. It was the fourth day of our journey – having travelled first through Slovakia and then the General Gouvernement[5], towards a still unknown destination. This was the first transport of Hungarian Jews[6] sentenced to be exterminated.

The Tatra mountains were now behind us. So too were Lublin and Krakow. During the war both these towns[7] became associated with the concentration and annihilation of anti-Fascists from the whole of Europe, brought to these occupied territories by representatives of the 'New Order'.

An hour after leaving Krakow, our train stopped at a larger station. The Gothic sign told us that we had arrived at a place called 'Auschwitz'. The name meant nothing to us. We had never heard of it before.

Through a crack in the boxcar wall I was able to observe a great commotion outside. Our SS escort were disembarking and being replaced by new guards on the train. The train staff was also leaving. From snatches of conversations it could be surmised that we had arrived at our destination.

The wagons moved once more, but after twenty minutes the train again ground to a halt.

I found the crack through which I could once again observe the world outside. We were now in a monotonously flat area. The ground was yellowish from the clay, so typical of eastern Silesia. The monotony of the terrain was only interrupted here and there by green clumps of trees. In front of me, however, there was a vast enclosure stretching all the way to the horizon; concrete posts at regular intervals with barbed wire stretched between them. Porcelain insulators and numerous high voltage signs made it clear that the wire fences were electrified. The concrete posts marked out huge rectangles, within which I could see hundreds of green barracks covered with roofing felt, and in between them long, straight streets.

Behind the wires I could also see figures dressed in striped prison uniforms. A group of them was carrying planks, another was proceeding in a column with shovels slung over their shoulders. A bit farther on, heavy logs were being loaded onto some lorries. And all around the enclosure, every 30 or 40 metres, stood some very characteristic, one-storey structures: watchtowers. In each there was a man in a field grey SS uniform, leaning on a machinegun.

This was Auschwitz concentration camp[8], or as the Germans, who love abbreviations, called it: KZ (katset).

It was a menacing sight. Yet for the time being, curiosity and tense expectation suppress the fear within me.

I looked round at my fellow travellers in the carriage: 26 physicians, eight pharmacists, our wives and children and a few elderly men and women – my colleagues' parents. Visibly tired, they sat despondently on their bundles of belongings or on the floor. Perhaps a premonition of what was going to happen next had prevented them from being jolted out of their apathy by the agitating moment of arrival. Most of the children were asleep, though some were eating what was left of the food, usually just bread. There were also those who had already run out of bread and were now licking their parched lips with equally dry little tongues.

The sound of sand sifting beneath heavy boots and the shouting of orders rudely interrupted our silent anticipation. The padlocks were unlocked and the doors slid open with a clatter. Then the first order was yelled out: 'Leave your suitcases and packages behind, just take your hand luggage!' The men – some holding infants in their arms – helped their wives and children to disembark the boxcar onto a ramp which was one and a half metres below. We were immediately made to line up in front of the wagons.

Before us stood a young SS officer with shiny knee boots and golden rosettes on his epaulettes. It is clear that he was the one giving the orders to the other SS-men. I was not yet familiar with SS insignia, but I knew from the Aesculapian symbol on his arm that he was a physician. I was to discover later that this was an SS *Hauptsturmführer*. His name: Dr Mengele, the chief physician of Auschwitz concentration camp[9], who was present on the ramp whenever a new transport arrived, for he was in charge of carrying out the selections[10].

Then it began! The SS-men hurriedly separated the men from the women and children. Anyone under fourteen was to remain with their mothers. Thus the long column of people standing in front of the train was being divided into two groups. Naturally, there was consternation. We were being immediately separated from our families. The guards answered our questions in calm voices:

'There's no need to be alarmed,' they said. 'You're going off to be bathed now, and disinfected – that's the procedure here. And then you'll all be reunited with your families.'

In the time it took to separate a group of four thousand people[11] I was able to have a look round. The light of the setting sun dramatically extruded the landscape that I had previously glimpsed at through a crack in the boxcar wall. Now I could see much more. The first thing that caught my eye, and left me riveted, was a huge redbrick chimney, square shaped and tapering slightly at the top. It was part of a formidable two-storey edifice[12], also of red brick and looking like some kind of a factory. This was a most peculiar factory chimney, however. To my astonishment, it was spewing out a column of fire a few metres into the air. There were lighting rods at each of its four corners. I was trying to image what kind of hell's kitchen required such an immense blaze and the answer came to me quickly. It was a crematorium! A bit further on I noticed another. Then I spotted a third, hidden behind some trees. All had flames coming out of their chimneys[13]. A gentle wind blew the smoke in our direction. My nostrils filled with the nauseous pungency of burning hair and meat. Burning flesh produces acrolein, whose odour resembles the smell of church candles made of low-quality animal fat.

I could have gone on reflecting on all these impressions for a long time, but the next stage of selection had already begun. Men, women and children were made to walk past the commission in single file. With a hand gesture from the selecting physician, henceforth referred to as Dr Mengele, we were once again divided into two groups; some went to the left, others to the right. I noticed that, apart from the women with children under fourteen years old, the people going to the left were mainly old or those who looked decrepit, infirm and very tired. The group forming on the right comprised people who looked fit for work. I noticed my wife and fourteen-year-old daughter had also joined this group. We were no longer able to communicate verbally but we could still wave to one another.

Some Red Cross vans collected the seriously ill, the very old and infirm, and the mentally handicapped. A few of my colleagues, elderly doctors, asked to be given a lift and were also loaded onto one of the vehicles. The motorised column moved off first. It was followed by the group on the left; they proceeded in fives at a slow pace, escorted by several SS-men. A few minutes later they disappeared behind a clump of trees. The group on the right stayed put.

Then Dr Mengele ordered all physicians from this group to step forward. He approached the fifty or so physicians and said he was looking for someone who had completed studies at a German university, had expert knowledge of carrying out post-mortems and was familiar with forensic medicine.

'You have to have genuine qualifications, or else ...' Here he made a very telling gesture.

I looked round at my colleagues. Was there no one else among them with such qualifications? Perhaps they felt intimidated by the threat? No one was coming forward. I, on the other hand, had already made up my mind. What the hell! I broke away from the rest to stand in front of Dr Mengele and tell him my name. The questions that followed were meticulous: Where had I studied? Where and under which professor had I learnt to perform autopsies? Which authority had granted me the right to practise forensic medicine? How long was my work experience in this field? Et cetera, et cetera. My answers must have satisfied him because he soon ordered me to stand to one side. My colleagues were ordered to rejoin the rest of the group on the right; then they were all ordered to march off. They had received a temporary stay of execution: they went down the road leading to the camp. Though I did not yet know it then, as I do now, a few minutes after setting off the group on the left passed through a gate leading to one of the crematoria, from which they would never return.

II

I was now standing on the ramp alone, aware of what ultimately awaited us. I was thinking about Germany, where I had spent so many years, the most beautiful years of my youth. Stars began to appear in the sky. High, high up the Big Dipper came into view straight above my head – just like at home in Nagyvárad. The now cooler evening breeze would have refreshed me were it not carrying with it the stench of Third Reich crematoria; the smell of burning corpses and acrolein.

Hundreds of glaring arc lights mounted on concrete posts now dazzled my eyes. Beyond this chain of brilliant light the air seemed to stand still, like a thick fog enveloping the faint silhouettes of the camp barracks in a heavy veil of darkness.

The ramp was now virtually empty, the stillness was only disrupted by a few prisoners in striped uniforms who were taking the abandoned luggage from the wagons and loading it onto lorries. The empty wagons, which not so long ago had been so much a part of our fate, were gradually fading from view in the twilight.

Dr Mengele gave some final instructions to SS subordinates and then headed for his Opel car. Having seated himself behind the steering wheel, he then indicated for me to get in too. On the back seat next to me sat an SS non-commissioned officer. The car moved.

We drove down a clay, camp road which was very uneven in places after the spring rains. The brilliant lights of the barbed wire perimeter streaked by. It was a short journey, and soon we stopped in front of a closed gate. Another SS non-commissioned officer immediately emerged from the *Blockführerstube*, that is the camp guardhouse, and obediently opened the gate to let Dr Mengele's car through. We drove on another few hundred metres down the camp's main street, which was flanked by barracks on either side, and stopped in front of a building that stood out from the rest.

Dr Mengele got out. I followed him. There was just enough time for me to read the sign at the door: '*Schreibstube*'. We entered. Behind some desks sat men in striped uniforms; they had intelligent faces. Without a word, all of them immediately rose to attention.

Dr Mengele turned to one of them, a man of about fifty with a shaven head. I was standing a few metres away, and so was unable to make out what they were saying. The senior physician at camp F [BIIf][14], Dr Senkteller [Roman Zenkteller – FP] for that was the prisoner's name as I was later to discover – nodded his head. Then he beckoned me a to a desk behind which sat another inmate. I was requested to give my personal details, which were recorded in a large register and onto an index card. The index card was next given to the SS non-commissioned officer escorting me and we left. As we passed Dr Mengele I instinctively bowed my head slightly; in response to which Dr Zenkteller commented, with irony rather than malice, that this was a KZ, not a salon.

We got as far as the third barracks, above which was another sign: Bath and Disinfection I was handed over, along with my card, to another SS-man. Two men in prisoner uniforms approached me. They searched my pockets and ordered me to undress. Then a barber arrived and shaved off all my hair. Next I was ordered to get under a shower. They smothered me with a calcium chloride, which stung so much that for several minutes I was unable to open my eyes. In yet another chamber I received a grey jacket and black trousers in place of the clothes I had taken off. However, I was returned my shoes, once they had been soaked in a tub of the said chlorine solution. As I was getting dressed I wondered about the fellow inmate the clothes had once belonged to.

One of the prisoners pulled up my left sleeve and, referring to the index card, proceeded to very skilfully and quickly perforate innumerable times the skin on my forearm with and instrument resembling a ball-point pen. Blue spots spread out from the points where my skin had been pricked. The prisoner comforted me that the inflammation would quickly pass and then the figures on my skin would be clear and legible. So Dr Miklós Nyiszli had ceased to exist. I was now merely number A 8450[15], a concentration camp prisoner. At that moment I recalled a situation from fifteen years before when the Dean of Frederick Wilhelm University in Breslau officially handed me my degree and, shaking my hand, wished me every success in the future.

III

I found myself in a strange emotional state. However, there had never been room in my life for passiveness or despair, so now too I had to adapt to the new situation... No, I would not fall into despair. I couldn't afford to be sentimental; I couldn't afford to be weak. Moreover, I also realised that for the time being my situation was not so bad. Dr Mengele needed my skills as a physician. I was most probably going to be sent to a town to partially or fully take over from some German forensic doctor who had been called up by the German Army. What convinced me of this was the fact that – no doubt on Dr Mengele's instructions – I had been given elegant civilian clothes instead of a prison uniform. One could deduce from that that my future job would require me to be presentable. Of course, this was merely a hypothesis. I had no way of telling what the real future held in store!

Yet another SS guard, with my index card in his hand, escorted me out of the building to the barracks opposite, No.12. The building was about 100 metres long. Inside there was a long corridor with three-tier bunks on either side constructed of rough logs and planks, and these bunks were crammed full of sick prisoners. I was in Block 12 of the hospital camp F [BIIf].

The SS-man handed the index card to an elderly, chubby-faced prisoner who had hurried to meet us. The prisoner stood to attention before receiving the card. Once the SS-man had gone, I shook hands with the prisoner and we introduced ourselves. It turned out that he was the block overseer. He led me to a small compartment screened off from a much larger room and asked me to sit down. As is the custom with convicts, he began to tell me his life history.

This was a Third Reich citizen: a *Reichsdeutsch*. Fifty years old, in 'civilian life' he used to be a safe-cracker. He claimed he always worked alone. His last 'job' had been a major one: he had broken into the vaults of a Düsseldorf bank at noon. He was able to live off the loot for three years until his estranged wife gave him away. He was given ten years at Moabit Prison. The sentence served, he was released only to find the Gestapo waiting for him outside the prison gate. He was immediately sent to Auschwitz concentration camp. That was four years ago.

There was a white patch sewn onto his striped uniform just above the heart with a green triangle and some numbers. At a concentration camp a green triangle meant that the bearer was a criminal category prisoner. He explained to me the system of marking prisoners. A red triangle meant the wearer was a political prisoner; lilac coloured triangles were worn by Bible Readers (Jehovah's Witnesses). Vagabonds and prostitutes had black triangles. Pink was for homosexuals, who were prosecuted under Article 175[16].

It was already past midnight and I should have been very tired, but my curiosity kept me awake. I listened intently to the block overseer's every word. He had extremely valuable insight into the whole, complex, organisational structure of this concentration camp. He knew the names of all the *Lagerführers*[17] in each of the camp sections. He knew the '*prominents*': prisoners who had special privileges and special functions. I discovered that Auschwitz concentration camp was not a labour camp but the Third Reich's largest extermination factory. I listened to his description of weekly selections in barracks and camp hospitals, after which the victims were loaded onto lorries and driven to the crematoria several hundred metres away.

From his account a clear picture emerged of life at the camp. Tens of thousands of prisoners were concentrated in barracks, in confined areas, which would be even too small to cage animals: These people were allowed only very little sleep, resting on each others heads, backs and legs, in terrible misery.

Night silence ended at three in the morning, just before dawn. Functionary prisoners woke their wretched fellow inmates with truncheons. They were all driven out of the barracks and made to stand in rank and file. Thus began one of the most inhuman items on the concentration camp's daily schedule: roll call... The prisoners stood in ranks five deep. One functionary inmate would arrange them so that the tallest prisoners stood in the first rank and the shortest ones in the last rank. Then another functionary would come along and trash the prisoners with his truncheon, so that the shortest ones moved to the very front and the tallest ones went to the very back. Finally the block overseer would emerge from the barracks, well fed, in newly washed and ironed uniforms. He would adopt a Napoleonic pose in front of the ranks of prisoners and vigilantly observe them to spot anything that might displease him. And, of course, something always did! He then immediately sprang into action, flaying out with clenched fists, knocking down several bespectacled men from the front rank, and then proceeding to push and shove them to the rear ranks. Why? No one knew. No one even asked that question. Here, in the concentration camp, no one even tried to understand the reason for persecuting others, and no explanations were forthcoming from the persecutors either.

All this lasted for hours on end. Frequently, prisoners could be counted and recounted in reverse order, moved from the front to the back and then *vice versa* as many as fifteen times. If one of the lines wasn't straight, all the inmates of the barracks were made to crouch with arms raised for half an hour. Their legs would wobble from exhaustion. Mornings at Auschwitz were chilly, even in summer. The thin cotton uniforms offered no protection against the rain or the cold. Moreover, roll call always began at dawn and did not end before 7, when the SS-men arrived.

The block overseer was usually a servile lackey of the SS. At almost every block the post was held by a thug with a green triangle. He would always stand to attention when reporting the number of prisoners at the block. The SS *Blockführer* also reviewed the front rank, counted the prisoners standing in file and then registered their number in his notebook. If anyone from the block had died – and, indeed, there were usually five, or six, or sometimes even ten corpses – they were also included in the roll call. The deceased lay at the very back, for while roll call lasted, the number of prisoners in a particular block had to tally, regardless of whether they were alive or dead. Sometimes, when there was a particularly large number of prisoner deaths, the man-pulled cart collecting the bodies wouldn't turn up for two or three days. Then the corpses had to be present at every roll call until they were eventually removed and could be crossed off the register.

After hearing all this from the block overseer, I no longer regretted my decision. I had had the courage to respond to Dr Mengele's inquiry, and thus had avoided what would otherwise have also been my fate. I had taken on the job he intended for a physician. I would not be swallowed up by the barracks and quarantine camp. Thanks to my civilian clothes I retained the outward appearance of a human being, and that night I would sleep in a bed with sheets in the doctors' room of Block 12.

Here, reveille was at seven in the morning. The physicians, including myself, and the entire hospital staff assembled outside the barracks. The SS checked the number of those present, but it didn't last longer than two or three minutes. They also counted all the sick prisoners in the cubicles, including those who had died in the night. Their bodies had to lie beside those who were still alive.

We ate breakfast in the doctors' room, where I got to know my colleagues. The *Leitenderarzt*[18] of Block 12 was Dr Levy, a Strasbourg University professor. His assistant was Dr Grosz, a Zagreb

University professor. Both were internists whose research findings had made them renowned throughout Europe.

Ignoring the danger and the fatigue, ignoring their own tragedy, without medical equipment, without medicines, without the means to disinfect or sterilise dressings, they tried to treat and relieve of pain the victims of Auschwitz, where even the fittest body could break down after four or five weeks of hunger, dirt, insects and murderously hard labour. And what then could be said of those who were already sick, who already had physical disorders when they arrived! My colleagues were extraordinary people and extraordinary doctors in a place where it is difficult enough to remain human, let alone be a good physician.

The example of these two remarkable doctors was enthusiastically followed by a six-man team of physicians. They included kind and sympathetic doctors from France and Greece. For three years now they had been eating camp bread: baked chestnut flour with an addition of sawdust. Their parents, wives and children were exterminated immediately after their arrival. Even those kinfolk who were told to join the column on the right did not survive longer than three or four months, and were eventually selected from their blocks to go to the crematorium.

These physicians were fully aware of the atrociousness, hopelessness of there own fate. Yet despite this, they devotedly tried to help others who were about to die. For the hospital patients were practically dead. You had to be really seriously ill to end up in a concentration camp hospital... Skin and bones weighing no more than 30 kilograms, virtual skeletons; the bodies covered with extensive phlegmons, lips swollen from hunger, yellow-skinned shadows of men suffering from interminable diarrhoea – such were the camp hospital patients. These were the people a camp physician had to save!

IV

I hadn't as yet been assigned a job, so one of the French doctors showed me round section F [BIIf]. The first thing that caught my eye was a wooden shed annexed to Block 12. Inside there was a rough table made of planks that hadn't been planed, a single chair and behind it a wooden box with segments containing instruments for dissecting bodies; and there was also a zinc bucket in the corner. That was the entire contents of this shed. My colleague explained that this was the hospital camp's only dissecting room, but it hadn't been used for a long time. Currently the camp had no specialist who could perform dissections. I realised that it was quite probable that my presence here had something to do with reactivating this dissecting room – after all, Dr Mengele clearly intended to set up such a unit.

My illusions were shattered. I had imagined that I would be performing autopsies in a modern, fully equipped dissecting room, not a crude camp shed. In my past work experience I had been called out to many a backwater to dissect exhumed bodies or the bodies of people who were murdered or had committed suicide, but I had never had to work with such inadequate equipment in such primitive conditions.

Of course, I quickly came to terms with the situation – such is my nature. The only thing I didn't understand was why I'd been given new civilian clothes to work in such a vile, dirty shed? There was a deeper significance in this contradiction, but I couldn't put my finger on it just yet.

My companion and I peered through the fence of another enclosure. The adjacent camp section was swarming with naked, swarthy children running around and having fun. There were colourfully dressed women with beautiful Creole features and men stripped to the waist, both young and old, all together in the same enclosure, sitting on the ground, standing in groups, talking or just watching the children play.

This was the famous 'Gypsy camp'[19]. Third Reich racists had declared Gypsies to be a lower category of people, and as such, they posed a threat to the purity of the Germanic race. Consequently, they had been rounded up from all territories under German control and deported here. They were granted the privilege of living together with their families because they were Catholics. The old, the young and children lived within the enclosure wherever they pleased. There were about 4,500 of them in all. They did not have to work, but were assigned the job of policing the neighbouring Jewish camps and barracks, where they exercised their authority with unimaginable cruelty.

The Experimental Barracks was the 'curiosity' of the Gypsy camp. The laboratory there was headed by Dr Bertolt Epstein, a professor of Prague University and world-famous paediatrician. He had been a concentration camp prisoner for four years now. His assistant, an associate professor of the Medical Academy in Paris, was Dr Bendel.

The research was carried out in three areas. First, the then fashionable subject of twins, which had become increasingly popular since the birth of quintuplets in Canada. Second, the physiology and pathology of stunted growth in people. Third, the possible causes and methods of treating *noma faciei* – a kind of gangrene of the face and mouth. This terrible disease is normally very rare and only occurs in isolated cases. In the Gypsy camp, however, one could speak of an outbreak of noma among the children. And apparently the research was already producing results. A great part of the Gypsy child sufferers also had inherited syphilis. There was no doubt that typhus, diphtheria, scarlet fever, the measles and malnutrition all contributed to the condition. However, these diseases were equally common among children in the Czech, Polish and Jewish camps, and yet there they did not lead to the development of the gangrene. The inference of this was that the chief cause of the disease was syphilis... This finding contradicted what had until then been conventional wisdom in the medical establishment, namely that noma mainly appeared in association with the measles, scarlet fever and typhus.

Dr Mengele visited the experimental barracks every day. He participated with great interest in the studies alongside the two renowned doctors and the painter Dina, whose extraordinary artistic talents enabled her to produce the diagrams and drawings necessary to illustrate the findings. She had arrived at the camp from Prague three years before. As Dr Mengele's worker, she had also acquired a privileged position at Auschwitz.

V

As chief physician at Auschwitz concentration camp, Dr Mengele was indefatigable. He spent hours at the experimental barracks in the Gypsies camp, and then spent half the time on the Jewish ramp, where currently four or five transports of deportees were arriving from Hungary every day.

The newcomers slowly approached the camp in long columns, in fives, flanked by the SS. I observed from afar; the elegant cloths, trench coats and fashionable bags told me that they were probably from one of the major cities.

Dr Mengele could even manage the time to deal with me personally. A long cart pulled by prisoners drew up in front of the dissecting chamber. The *Kommando* assigned the job of collecting the dead unloaded two corpses from the back of the vehicle. They had the letters ZS written on their chest with blue ink: ZS stood for *zur Sektion*, which meant for dissection.

One of the French prisoners from Block 12 – an intelligent man – served as my assistant. We laid the bodies on the table. There was a strong, black cord noosed around the neck of one of them: the prisoner had hanged himself or had been hanged by someone else. I took a cursory look at the other corpse and immediately saw that the cause of death must have been electrocution. It was easy to recognise by the small circular burns with reddish-violet fringes. Here again I tried to guess which of the two possibilities was the actual cause of death. Had the hapless prisoner thrown himself on to the electrified fence or had he been thrown? Both scenarios frequently occurred in the camp.

The formalities here, however, did not require these questions to be answered. Regardless of whether someone had committed suicide, simply died or had been murdered, his name was crossed off the register, while his body was throw onto a cart and taken to the mortuary. Every day forty to fifty corpses were taken there. Then in the evening a lorry conveyed them to one of the crematoriums.

Dr Mengele had sent me the two bodies as a test. From the outset he had warned me to be very careful and that I would have to fulfil all his requirements.

The roar of a car engine. 'Attention!' the sonorous command rang out in Block 12. Dr Mengele had arrived, accompanied by two high ranking SS officers. They listened to the reports of the block overseer and block physician and then went straight to the dissecting room, where an autopsy was about to be performed. All the physicians from camp F [BIIf] follow them, as if this was going to be a post-mortem examination at a great institute and the subject was a particularly interesting case. I could see the tension on their faces and also curiosity to discover how this candidate would fare before such a dangerous examiner. I felt that my fellow doctors were worried about me.

No one, apart from myself, knew that in my three years as assistant to Dr Strassman at the Breslau Institute of Forensic Medicine I had come across every conceivable case, including all forms of suicide. The knowledge I had acquired then was also the knowledge of camp physician No. A 8450.

I proceeded with the autopsy. I opened up the skull, chest and abdomen and remove all the internal organs, pointing out what tissue changes had occurred. At the same time I was being bombarded with numerous questions and replying to each of them immediately. The doctors' tense faces relaxed, the uncertainty had vanished and was replaced by glances of admiration which were a sign that the exam was going well. I went on to dissect the next body. Doctor Mengele ordered me to write a report of my findings. He would send someone round for the documentation the next day. The SS doctors left. I started talking with my fellow prisoners. So far they'd only been polite, but now I felt I'd been accepted as part of their team.

The next day I was given three more bodies to dissect. The audience was exactly the same as before, but the atmosphere was no longer so tense. More questions were asked, some provoking lively discussions.

Once the SS doctor had left, several young French and Greek physicians approached me. They asked me to explain to them the technique of performing the lumbar puncture and allow them to practise it on corpses. I willingly agreed, feeling touched that even here, behind concentration camp barbed wire, they wished to further their knowledge. They persevered and on their fifth or sixth attempt succeed in performing a proper lumbar puncture, then withdrew, quite pleased with their afternoon's work.

VI

It was the third day and I still hadn't been assigned a job. Nonetheless, I was receiving a physician's food rations. I rested on my bed in the doctors' room or sat out on a bench by a football pitch that was adjacent to the blocks. Yes, there was even a sports field at Auschwitz concentration camp. However, only privileged prisoners were allowed to use it – usually Germans. On Sundays football matches were played there. On other days it stood empty. Just a single barbed-wire fence separated the sports field from Crematorium I.[20] I very much wanted to know what went on behind the walls of that building with the blazing chimney. There wasn't much to see from where I was sitting, but it would have been foolish to come any closer to the perimeter. Whoever did would immediately encounter a hail of machinegun bullets from one of the many watchtowers.

I had just enough time to observe a column of men in civilian clothes lining up in front of the redbrick block. There were some two hundred of them. Several SS-man stood in front of the column. I surmised that there was some kind of roll call going on there. The crematorium workers were presumably changing shifts – the night shift was probably replacing the day shift. I knew from one of the more experienced inmates that the prisoner squad at the crematorium was called the *Sonderkommando*, which meant a *Kommando* for special tasks. The members were well fed, they walked in the best civilian clothes and... performed the worst job. They were never allowed to leave their *Kommando*. Every three

26

or four months, when it was deemed that they knew too much, they were liquidated. That had been the case with every *Kommando* so far[21]. Ever since the setting up of a concentration camp in Oświęcim (Auschwitz) no one had come out alive to tell the world of what had been going on for years within those terrible walls.

I returned to Block 12 just in time to meet Doctor Mengele. He had arrived by car and was being greeted by the block overseer. They beckoned me to join them. Doctor Mengele ordered me to get inside his car, this time without a guard. I wasn't given the time to say farewell to my friends. We drove off, but soon stopped in front of the camp office. Doctor Mengele ordered Dr Zenkteller, who was hurrying in our direction, to fetch my index card. A few seconds later he already had it in his hand.

We drove on for ten minutes down a road flanked by barbed wire enclosures and through the heavily guarded gates of the various camp sections. Only now did I see how huge this concentration camp was. The vast majority of inmates never got the opportunity to see the whole camp; most died in the camp section they had arrived at. My observations were unexpectedly interrupted by Dr Mengele. Without turning his head round, he declared: 'I'm not taking you to a sanatorium, but you'll find it quite bearable there.'

We left the camp and drove some 300 metres along an unloading ramp. The car slowed down and Mengele honked the horn. A huge iron gate in the wire enclosure opened. There were guards at the gate. We drove on to a spacious green lawn courtyard. The gravel paths and the green poplars would have made this place seem quite cosy were it not for the redbrick building with its chimney throwing out flames. This was the premises of one of the crematoria. We got out of the car. An SS-man approached us and reported to Dr Mengele. We went across the courtyard together and entered the crematorium building through a large doorway.

'Is the room ready?' Dr Mengele asked our SS guide. The SS-man answered in the affirmative, so we went straight there. I entered the room last.

I found myself in a newly whitewashed room. There was plenty of light coming in from a large window looking out on to the courtyard. However, the window had bars. After the camp barracks, the furnishing seemed quite luxurious: a white bed, white wardrobe, a long table and chairs. There was a red, plush cover on the table and some nice carpets on the concrete floor. All this suggested that my arrival had been expected. The people from the *Sonderkommando* must have painted the walls and then furnished the room with items off the transports, though bed and wardrobe had most probably been made at a camp workshop.

We next proceeded down a long dark corridor to another chamber. We found ourselves in a modern dissecting room, well illuminated by two windows. A red concrete floor, in the centre of which there was a concrete base supporting a grey marble slab with numerous drainage channels. There was a water basin attached to one end of the table, below some nickel taps. There were three porcelain washbasins against the walls, which had been painted light green with an oil-based paint. The large barred windows were covered with a fine mesh against mosquitoes and flies.

Moving on from the dissecting room, we entered the doctor's surgery: elegant, veneered furniture, comfortable armchairs, and in the centre of it, a long table covered with a grey tablecloth. On the table there were three microscopes. In one of the corners there was a huge wide bookcase containing the latest medical journals. There was also a glass cabinet full of various chemicals and a chest of draws containing white coats, aprons, towels and rubber gloves. Everything just like in a modern, pathology unit of a metropolitan institute.

As observed all this, the terror sank in. It dawned on me that the moment I had crossed the gate my fate was sealed. Now I understood why I had been given civilian clothes. Such clothes were warned by the *Sonderkommando*: the *Kommando* that was sentenced to die.

Doctor Mengele was preparing to leave. He instructed the SS-man that as far as my work was concerned I was answerable only to him. No one from the SS on the crematorium premises had the right to give me orders. My food was to be provided by the SS kitchen. I was allowed to take clothes and underwear from the storeroom. I was allowed to have my hair cut by the SS barber. I was not obliged to attend morning and evening roll calls. Apart from doing laboratory work and performing autopsies, I was also obliged to provide medical care for some 120 SS-men and 860 *Sonderkommando* prisoners[22]. I was to be provided with all the necessary medicines, instruments and dressings. I was obliged to treat all the sick on the crematorium premises and visit them on a daily basis. From 7 a.m. to 9 p.m. I was allowed to move around freely, that was without an escort, on the premises of all four crematoria. Every day I was to report to the commander of the crematorium SS and the *Sonderkommando – Obersharführer* Muhsfeldt[23] – the total number of bedridden and ambulant patients.

I listened to this long list of my rights and duties mortified. Under such conditions I should be KZ's most important figure, were I not in the Sonderkommando and were all this not taking place in the crematorium I.

Dr Mengele left without saying another word. No one from the SS, not even those of the lowest rank, ever said farewell to a concentration camp prisoner.

I closed the dissecting room door and put away the keys. All this was my responsibility now.

Having returned to my room, I sat down and tried to gather my thoughts. But it was so difficult! In my mind I saw my house. The sunny veranda, the pleasant rooms where I had spent so many happy days with my family. I also remembered my surgery, the many difficult hours spent there treating patients and the joy I experienced when my treatment helped. Where were my friends and family in this gigantic, anonymous prison? Was my fifteen-year-old daughter still with her mother? Had they managed to avoid getting separated? What had happened to my elderly parents, whom I had tried to surround with love and shelter from worries in the autumn of their lives? What had happened to my younger sister, a beautiful, delicate girl, for whom I had tried to take over the role of our sick father? I was so happy with all of them, I loved them and found joy in being able to look after them. Not for one moment did I have any illusions as to their fate: my father, mother and sister were already on one of the forty-wagon transports bound for Auschwitz. On the unloading ramp a single gesture from my boss, Dr Mengele, would direct my parents to join the column on the left. My sister would go there, too. With tears in her eyes, she'd beg to be allowed to join our mother. Permission would be granted, and my sister, touched by this apparent act of compassion, would thank them with sincere gratitude ...

News of my arrival had spread like wildfire among the members of both the SS staff and the *Sonderkommando*. I had numerous guests. The first to open the door were non-commissioned officers of the SS. Two very well built *Obersharführers* with gloomy demeanours entered my room. I realised that way I behaved now would affect the way these two would treat me in the future. I thought about what Dr Mengele had said: I was answerable only to him. I treated their arrival as a private and social call. Therefore I did not comply to the concentration camp regulations which would have required me to immediately rise to attention and report to them. I greeted them without getting up and invited them to sit down.

They stood in the middle of the room eyeing me carefully – I realised the importance of this moment. It's the first impressions that count. I was satisfied that I had assessed the situation well. I had passed another exam. The tension on the SS-men's faces was gone and they nonchalantly sat down. Our conversation was limited to a very narrow range of topics, such as enquiring about my journey here. However, they did not ask why I had been sent to a concentration camp. A prisoner was not allowed to talk about politics, the war or the prevailing mood within the camp. Despite these limitations, I did not feel awkward. The years I had spent in peacetime Germany had supplied me with a rich selection of topics for conversation.

My guests allowed themselves to be drawn into an actual discussion – perhaps impressed by the fact that I spoke their language with a greater eloquence than they themselves did. I used several expressions they did not even understand, though they did not admitted to it. I knew their country well: the cities, German family life, the nation's moral and religious principles. I felt convinced I had also passed the oral part of the exam. My visitors were satisfied and left.

The next guests to call on me were dressed in clean civilian clothes and clean-shaven. They included two *Kapos* and the *Oberkapo* of the *Sonderkommando*.[24] I learned that they were the ones who had had my room prepared. They had heard of my arrival and invited me to sup with them and meet the other prisoners. They had paid this visit so that we could become acquainted.

It was suppertime, so I left my room to go with them to the first floor of the crematorium building, where the crematorium staff lived. It was a huge corridor lined with comfortable, single beds on either side. The beds were made of untreated wood, but on each one silk coverlets and embroidered pillows shone. The array of lively colours clashed with the rest of the room. It was obvious that these various items had been taken off the transports. Prisoners of the *Sonderkommando* were at liberty to take from the storerooms whatever they pleased.

The lighting was far too bright. Electricity was not economised on here as it was in the camp barracks. We proceeded along a long row of beds. Only half the *Kommando* was there. The other half was now on the night shift. While they were working, the dayshift was resting. A few were already asleep. Others were reading books. There were plenty of books there. Almost every deportee thought of also taking something with him for the soul. Reading was another of the *Sonderkommando's* privileges. Any prisoner in the camp caught reading a book got 20 days in the bunker, that was if they didn't beat him into a pulp straight away.

Waiting for us was a dining table covered with a damask cloth. There were delicate porcelain plates bearing monograms, silver cutlery and fine porcelain jugs – all of it also from the transports. The table was laden with the good things that deportees had decided to take with them on their journey into the unknown: all sorts of tinned food, smoked pork fat, salami, fruit juice, biscuits and chocolate. From the labels I recognised these products and knew that they had originated from Hungary. Such perishables were left for those who had not yet perished: for the *Sonderkommando*. Taking their places at the table were the *Oberkapo*, the *Kapo* of the 'stokers' (meaning those who operated the crematorium ovens), the *Kapo* of the 'dentists', who remove teeth from the corpses, and the prisoner in charge of gold smelting. They offered me all they had, and there was an abundance of everything, for the Hungarian convoys continued to arrive at an over-increasing rate and they brought a great deal of food with them.

At first I found it difficult to swallow the food. I visualised my travelling companions, who in the final hours had clung on to their precious reserves with tears in their eyes. They would have rather starved during the journey than used up supplies intended at some critical moment for their children and elderly parents. The moment never came because the next day they were all dead... The untouched food remained in the crematorium's vestibule.

I sipped tea laced with rum. Soon I was quaffing it. After a few glasses the nervous tension eased. I had freed myself from those painful thoughts, I felt lighter, less inhibited. A pleasant warm sensation spread all over my body. That was the effect of alcohol. We smoked excellent cigarettes that had come from a Hungarian transport. The going price for a cigarette at the camp was one portion of bread! Here they were lying around on the table in cartons of a hundred.

There was a lively discussion going on now. Poland, France, Greece, Russia, Germany and Italy were all represented at the table. We spoke in German, as most of us knew this language.

In conversation I learnt the history of the crematoria. Tens of thousands of prisoners had built them out of stone and concrete. Despite the harsh winter weather, deadlines had to be met. Every stone had been stained with the blood of unfortunate Jewish prisoners. Hungry and cold, dressed in rags, fed with pigs' swill, these wretches had worked day and night to build a terrible death factory that would later turn their bodies to ash on the gridirons they themselves had installed. That had happened two years before. Since then millions of people had got off trains onto the ramp and passed through the crematorium gates.

I discovered the history of the *Sonderkommando*. This one was the twelfth. I listened to stories about leading personalities of previous *Sonderkommandos*, and heard confirmation of what had already been told to me in the camp – a *Sonderkommando* only lived several months.

Jewish believers had to start preparing for death, each in accordance with their particular religion, the moment they arrived here. For death was revocable. That had been the case with every *Sonderkommando* so far.

It was almost midnight and the alcohol had now made the *Sonderkommando* members languid. The conversation started to falter, start, then stop again. The SS-man on duty forewarned us that it was time we went to bed. I took my leave and returned to my room.

I slept soundly on my first night there: thanks to the potent rum, and thanks also to nervous exhaustion.

VII

The sustained siren call was coming from the ramp. It was early morning. I came up to window, which looked out directly onto the railway tracks. There was a long line of wagons on them now. It took a few minutes for the SS to slide open the doors, and out poured another transport, the chosen people of Israel. In under half an hour the assembling and selection process was over. The left column slowly moved off.

The loud yelling of orders and hurried footsteps reached my room. The noise was coming from the furnace room: they were preparing to receive the transport. Then came the murmur of generators and the whirr of huge ventilators starting up: the temperature in the ovens was being raised to the maximum level. There were over a dozen of these large fans, one to each oven, all working simultaneously. The place where the corpses were burnt was vast, with a concrete floor, whitewashed and full of light coming in from very large, barred windows. Each oven was individually encased in red brick. Massive iron doors, polished to shine, formed a row of black patches running along the whole interior.

It took five or six minutes for the transport to reach the gates. They swung open and, as usual, the column entered the courtyard in fives. No one else in the world knew what was about to happen next, for no one who had crossed the threshold ever returned. The road taken by the left column led to the crematorium, and not to the 'rest camp for the infirm, aged and very young', as the Germans had told those who had been deemed fit for work and were made to join the right-hand column.

34

The exhausted people proceeded very slowly. The children, half asleep, clung onto their mothers' dresses. The infants were held in their fathers arms. Some of the parents were pushing prams. The SS escort remained behind the gate. A notice warned them that access was denied to all unauthorised personnel, including the SS! The newly arrived immediately noticed the taps in the courtyard. They broke ranks and swarmed around them with their pots and pans in order to quench their terrible thirst. This mad, chaotic rush was hardly surprising: they had had virtually no water for the past five days and what little there had been to drink was stagnant. The SS guards who had now taken over were used to this scene and waited patiently for everyone to fill their vessels. Order could only be restored once everyone had quenched their thirst. Then the people slowly returned to their ranks. They proceeded another hundred metres or so down a gravel path leading to some iron railings where concrete steps took them underground into a concrete chamber. Before descending the steps they saw a large notice board informing them in German, French, Greek and Hungarian that this was a bathing and disinfecting facility. The sign reassured not only those who suspected nothing but also those who had been expecting the worst. They went down the steps almost joyfully.

The transport entered a spacious, whitewashed, brightly lit chamber, about 200 [50 – FP] metres long. There were columns running down the centre. Around the columns and beneath the walls on either side, benches. Above the benches, numbered coat hangers. Everywhere there were notices in various languages informing the newly arrived that they had to tie their clothes and shoes up in bundles, hang them on the hooks and memorise the coat hanger numbers in order to avoid unnecessary confusion when they returned from their bath. 'True German sense of order!' commented those who admired this particularly German attribute. And they were right! This was indeed all done for the sake of order, so that citizens waiting in the Reich did not get shoes that were mixed up. The same concerned the clothes – it was important that the bombed German people received them in good condition. There were 3000 people in the room. Men, women and children. Then the SS soldiers entered. The command was immediately given: 'Everyone is to undress.' And a time limit was set: 'Ten minutes!' The old, the children, husbands, wives all stood transfixed. The women and girls felt ashamed and looked around at each other helplessly. Perhaps they had misunderstood the German words? But the order was repeated. The voice was now impatient and menacing.

The people suspected something very bad was about to happen. Their first instinct was to resist. But after a while they gave in. Jews had grown accustomed to situations when they could be forced to do anything. Slowly they started to take their clothes off. The very old, the cripples and the mentally ill were assisted by members of the *Sonderkommando*. Within ten minutes everyone was naked. Their clothes were on the coat hangers, their shoes looked as if they were standing to attention. Everyone had memorised their coat hook number.

Some SS-men pushed their way through the dense crowd to a very wide, oak double door at the other end of the room. They opened both doors. The naked people thronged into the next chamber, which was also very brightly lit. The chamber was half the size of the undressing room. There were no benches or clothes hangers. Instead, in the centre there were some huge, four-sided pillars. These weren't supporting columns but enormous metal conduits with grates or a sort of latticework down their sides.

Everyone was now inside. A loud command rang out: 'SS and *Sonderkommando* to leave the room.' They left, making sure that none of their colleagues remained behind. The doors slammed shut, and then the lights in the shower room went out. Meanwhile in the courtyard one could hear the roar of an engine. A deluxe Red Cross ambulance arrived. An SS and an SDG officer (*Stanitätsdienstgehilfe* – a member of the SS auxiliary health service) got out. The latter held four green tins. They went across the lawn and stepped onto the shower room's flat, concrete roof, towards some low concrete chimneys. They approached the first one, and put on gas masks before proceeding to remove the chimney's heavy concrete cover. One of the tins was opened with a special patented device attached to it and its contents – greenish pellets the size of beans – was poured down the shaft. The crystals fell down the metal conduit into the underground shower room. They reached the bottom of the drain but did not spill out beyond it. This was Zyklon B. On contact with air it immediately began to vaporise. The gas seeped through the grates: within a few seconds it filled the chamber crammed full of people. Within five minutes the whole transport was dead.

The Red Cross ambulance arrived every time there was a new transport. The gas was brought in from somewhere outside. No full tins were ever held in the crematorium building. A clever precaution, but not half as clever and cynical as the precaution of marking the vehicle delivering the Zyklon B tins with the sign of the International Red Cross!

The two executioners who had delivered the lethal gas waited another five minutes to make sure they had done the job properly. Then they both lit up cigarettes and climbed back into the ambulance. They had just murdered three thousand people!

After twenty minutes the extractor fans were switched on to remove the gas. The doors opened. Some lorries pulled up. One of the *Sonderkommando* groups started loading the people's belongings. They separated the clothes from the shoes. They were to be taken for disinfecting. This time real disinfecting. From there the spoils would be sent out to various distribution centres in Germany.

The state of the art ventilators extracted the gas efficiently, but its residues still remained in various crevices in among the dead bodies. The inhaling of even a small quantity could cause choking, even after several hours. That was why another of the *Sonderkommando* squads, equipped with rubber hoses, entered the chamber wearing gas masks. The room was now once again brightly lit. The prisoners entering it encountered a ghastly sight.

The bodies did not lie scattered on the floor but were tangled, one on top of the other, in an incredibly tall, macabre pile. The gas emitted from the green crystals spread at ground level and then proceeded to rise higher and higher. Thus these unfortunates instinctively clambered up on top of one another to avoid inhaling it. Those highest up were the last to die. Such was the ghastly struggle for life that took place there. Life extended by one or two minutes! Were they still able to think straight, they would have understood the futility of trampling over their parents, wives and children; but they had stopped thinking, by then they were only driven on by the instinct of self-preservation. I observed that the infants lay at the very bottom, the children lay on top of them, then the women and the old, and on the very top the strongest men.

The corpses were entangled in mortal embraces, with bleeding noses and mouths, bodies scratched in the struggle to reach the top. Their faces pallid and swollen almost beyond recognition.

Despite this, members of the *Sonderkommando* did in fact frequently manage to identify their close ones in among the cadavers... an encounter I myself greatly dreaded.

There was no work for me there but, nevertheless, I went down to be among the dead. I had a duty towards my people and towards the entire world. If, by some incredible whim of fate, I were get out of that place alive – though at the time cold reason prohibited me from thinking that way – I could testify what my own eyes had seen.

The *Sonderkommando* squad, also wearing rubber boots, stood around the pile of corpses and hosed them down with powerful jets of water. One of the final effects of Zyklon B gassing before death was the emptying of the bowels – all the corpses were soiled.

Once 'the bathing of the dead' was done, the *Sonderkommando* proceeded, with great distress and self-abnegation, to disentangle the dead bodies from the pile. This was arduous work: thongs had to be used to grab the wet, clench-fisted corpses by the wrists, wrench them from the pyramid and then drag them to a lift in the next room. This was a large industrial lift which took twenty to twenty-five bodies at a time. A bell was rung when the lift was ready to go. The bodies were winched up to crematorium – the large lift doors opened automatically. There another *Sonderkommando* squad was already waiting for them. They once again used thongs to clasp the dead by their wrists and drag them over the concrete floor, down an already slippery path towards one of the fifteen fiery ovens.

The corpses of the old, the young and children lay in a long row on the concrete floor. The blood oozed out of their noses and mouths, and mingled with the water that continually flowed from open taps.

Now ensued the next act of profiting from murder. The Third Reich had already appropriated their clothes and footwear. But hair was also a valuable commodity and could be used in the delayed-action detonators of bombs. The dampness or dryness of air does not affect the moment of combustion for human hair. This fact ensures an exact timing of detonation. Thus the corpses' heads were shaved.

'Not gold but human work is the fortune of the Third Reich,' used to be one of the Nazi's slogans. Yet the truth of the matter was quite different. There were eight members of the 'Dentists' *Kommando*' standing in front of the ovens. Each held two instruments, or rather tools, in their hands: a chisel and a pair of pliers. They turned the corpses face-up and proceeded to do something appalling: they prised open the mouths and crudely broke off, rather than extracted, all the bridgework and gold teeth. Members of this *Kommando* were top-quality dentists and surgeons. Doctor Mengele had summoned these specialists to come forward under the pretence that he was planing to provide the camp with dental care. They had applied convinced that would be given tasks appropriate to their profession. Instead – like myself – they entered the crematorium hell.

The gold teeth were thrown into a bucket filled with hydrochloric acid, which dissolved away the pieces of meat and bone from the gold. Other items such as gold and platinum chains or rings were put into a special case that was always kept locked: they were thrown in through a slit in the lid. Gold is a heavy metal, my rough estimate was that every day each crematorium collected 8-10 kilos of gold – naturally it all depended on the transport. There were rich transports and there are poor transports, depending on where they had come from. The transports from Hungary arrived at the Auschwitz ramp already plundered. However, the people on the transports from Holland, the Reich Protectorate (Bohemia and Moravia) and Poland, despite the years they had spent in the ghettos, managed somehow to stow away their jewellery, gold and silver. And that was another way in which the Third Reich enriched itself.

Once the last gold tooth had been extracted, the victims were handed over to the *Kommando* in charge of the ovens. In teams of three they loaded the corpses onto special steel stretchers on wheels. The heavy, iron oven doors opened automatically. The prisoners pushed the stretchers towards the opening, tipped the corpses into the white-hot interior and immediately retreated. By then the stretchers were already red-hot and two prisoners using rubber hoses had to cool them down with powerful jets of water.

It took twenty minutes for a body to incinerate. The crematorium had fifteen ovens, all working at once. The daily output of a crematorium was five thousand human bodies. All four crematoria had the same output.[25] Every day twenty thousand people entered the gas chambers and eventually ended up in one of the ovens. Every day the souls of thousands of people were released through the crematorium chimneys. All that remained was a small pile of ash in the crematorium courtyard. The human ashes were loaded onto lorries and driven two kilometres to be dumped into the flowing waters of the Vistula.

After so much suffering and horror there was still no peace, even for the dead.

VIII

The laboratory and dissecting room had been set up at the wish of my boss, Doctor Mengele, to satisfy his scientific ambitions. In a few days everything had been completed and Doctor Mengele had only to wait for an autopsy specialist in order to begin his researches.

The concentration camp here opened up unlimited opportunities to perform anatomical and pathological examinations on the very numerous cases of suicide as well as research into the phenomena of twins and the growth disorders in both dwarfs and giants. There was no other place in the world where you could find so many bodies for dissection.

I knew from my own experience that the world's most renowned and largest clinics, institutes of forensic medicine and autopsy annually received no more than 100 to 150 bodies for dissection. At Auschwitz concentration camp, on the other hand, bodies available for 'research' ran into millions.

Anyone who crossed the camp gate could end up on the dissecting table. Those who by a mere twist of fate were directed to the left, ended up half an hour later in the gas chamber and became corpses. And those were actually the lucky ones. Those told to go to the right were sentenced to protracted agony. They, too, were candidates for the dissecting table, but they still had another three or four months to endure, in which time they would discover the whole horror of struggling for survival in a concentration camp. They would be crushed by the burden of slave labour, bleed from a thousand wounds, wither from hunger, freeze out in the fields. They'd lose their minds, howl and roll their eyes like madmen. Trained guard dogs would gnaw at what little flesh they'd have left. And once they were reduced to just skin and bone, and even the lice no longer had anything to feed on, only then did death come to liberate them. So who from among the fathers, mothers, brothers, sisters and children had the better lot: those who went to the right or those who went to the left?

When a new transport disembarked onto the ramp and the people started file up, one of the SS-men immediately approached them in search of twins and dwarfs. Mothers expected this to be something good for their children and handed them over without hesitation. The older ones assumed that by being twins they were an interesting subject for scientific research and that could only be to their advantage, so they volunteered. The dwarfs thought likewise.

The twins and dwarfs were therefore separated from the rest and went to the right side of the platform. SS guards escorted this particular group to a special barracks. There these prisoners received good food, comfortable beds, the necessary hygienic facilities and favourable treatment from the warders.

This was Block 14 of Camp F [BIIf], whence the prisoners were escorted to the aforementioned experimental block in the Gypsy camp and it was there that they were subjected to all the medical examinations that could possibly be performed on a living human being. Blood tests, lumbar punctures, blood transfusions between twins and innumerable other experiments; all very painful and exhausting. The painter form Prague, Dina, made comparative drawings of the twins heads, ears, noses, lips, arms and legs. Each drawing ended up in a special file along with all the personal details as well as all the findings of the experiments that had been carried out. The same procedure applied to the dwarfs.

These experiments were carried out – under the pretence of medical examinations – *in vivo*, that is on living organisms, and were in no way able to fully explain the phenomenon of twins from the scientific point of view. They were superficial, revealing very little on the subject. It was therefore necessary to move on to the next, most important phase of research: the post-mortem examination and the comparison of normal organs with ones that were malformed or simply sick. Such examinations required corpses. Because general autopsies and examinations of particular organs had to be carried out simultaneously, the twins in the experimental barracks of section D [BIId]] died simultaneously: Doctor Mengele killed them.

It was here that unique medical opportunities occurred: twins died at the same time, making it possible to carry out comparative autopsies. Could this have happened anywhere else in the world? Was it not close to a miracle to have a pair of twins die simultaneously with the subsequent possibility of dissecting both of their bodies?! Circumstance usually separates twins. They usually live tens or even hundreds of kilometres away from each other. It is normally impossible to carry out comparative autopsies of twins. At Auschwitz, however, there were hundreds of twins and if they were killed, there were hundreds of research opportunities.

That was why Dr Mengele searched for twins and dwarfs on the ramp. That was why they went to the right side and were taken to a 'good' barracks. For a time each pair received better food and were allowed to wash, so that neither of them succumbed to any illness or died too soon. They could only die together, in full health and at the same time!

The *Oberkapo* of the *Sonderkommando* came to inform me that there was an SS-man waiting for me at the crematorium gate. He was with a group of prisoners carrying bodies for me to dissect. I went out to meet them, for as non-crematorium staff both the prisoners and the SS-man were prohibited from even entering the courtyard. The SS-man handed me a file. It contained documents concerning a pair of twins. The *Kommando*, comprising women prisoners, placed before me a covered stretcher. I lifted the sheet to see beneath it the bodies of two-year-old twins. I told my people to take the stretcher to the dissecting room and place the bodies on the table.

I opened the file and examined the documents. They included scientific reports on both twins together with x-rays, drawings and professional medical data. Only the autopsy reports were missing. That was my job!

The two little children had died at the same time. Their tiny bodies lay on the huge dissecting table. Their deaths had made it possible for their bodies to be dissected and thus contribute in the search for a solution to the mystery of reproduction of the race.

'The great goal' of all this research was to increase the birth rate of 'super humans' who were destined to become the 'master race'. More specifically this would in the future mean every German mother giving birth to twins.

This scheme was sheer madness! It was the invention of the sick minds of Third Reich, the racist theoreticians. And the task of carrying out the research required to support it had been taken up by Doctor Mengele, the *Standortarzt* of Auschwitz concentration camp, a highly qualified '*Kriminal-doktor*', an evil doctor.

This was the most dangerous type of criminal, one who also had incredible power at his disposition. He was able to send millions to their death because German racial theory stated that these people were not really humans but an inferior species that had a harmful effect on humanity.

This same criminal would spend hours sitting beside me in among the microscopes, test tubes and flasks or standing at the dissecting table in a bloodstained apron examining and rummaging with bloodstained hands. All for the sake of increasing the procreation of the Germanic race, so that ultimately there would be enough Germans to populate the Third Reich's *Lebensraum* territories. That was, once they had been cleared of Czechs, Hungarians, Poles, the Dutch and other nations.

The autopsies of the twins were finished and I set about recording all my observations in the book. I could see that Mengele was pleased with my work but he had some difficulty with reading my handwriting, as it resembled printed text – I had learnt to write that way in America. I suggested that if he wanted my reports to be more legible, he could use a typewriter, as I had done at home.

'What make are you familiar with?' he asked.

'Olympia Elite,' I answered.

'No problem. You'll get it tomorrow. I'll send someone round. I require top-quality documentation, because it is going to the Institute of Anthropological, Biological and Racial Research in Berlin-Dahlem.'

It was then I discovered that the research was be overseen by outstanding scientists of one of the most renowned medical institutes.

The next day an SS-man brought me an Olympia typewriter. I also received more corpses. Four pairs of twins from the Gypsy camp. They were all children below the age of ten.

I proceeded to dissect the first pair of twins and progressively record each stage of the autopsy. I removed the top of the skull and took out the brain together with the cerebellum, so that both could be examined in detail. Next I opened up the ribcage and extracted the sternum. By making an incision below the chin, I was able to remove the tongue and oesophagus. These organs were very bloody and they had to be rinsed before I could examine them properly; after all, even the tiniest spot or discoloration could have considerable significance. Subsequently I opened up the pericardium and collected the exuded fluid. I removed the heart and rinsed off the blood under a running tap. Turning the heart around in my hand I noticed a tiny pale red, barely distinguishable spot the size of a pinprick on the exterior of the left ventricle. I had to be sure, but I wasn't mistaken: this was a very delicate mark left by a needle, it was the mark of a hypodermic needle insertion. Why had this child received an injection straight into the heart? Such injections are usually only given when there is sudden heart failure. The question was about to be answered. During autopsies we usually measure the amount of blood in the left ventricle. In this case, however, it turned out to be impossible, for the blood had coagulated into one solid clot. I extracted the clot with a pair of tweezers and sniffed it. I was hit by the characteristic, pungent smell of chloroform. The child had been injected with chloroform.

I was so nervous that my knees started trembling. I had discovered one of the darkest medical secrets of the Third Reich: innocent people were not only being killed with gas but also by being given lethal chloroform injections straight into the heart! Beads of sweat appeared on my forehead. Thankfully I was on my own. It would have been difficult for me to hide my emotions in front of other people. I finished the autopsy and recorded the anomalies. The only things I did not mention in the report were the needle mark on the left ventricle and the blood clot. This was out of caution. I had in my hands Dr Mengele's files on the twins. They too contained precise medical data, various findings, x-rays and drawings. However, the cause of death was not mentioned. That space on the forms was left empty. My report also did not state the cause of death. It would have been very imprudent of me to write down all my findings. I was not a coward. I had strong nerves. In my life, I had conducted many autopsies and discovered innumerable causes of death. I had examined the bodies of people who had been murdered out of revenge, out of jealousy or for profit. I had established the way in which people had committed suicide and identified diseases that had been the cause of death for others. I had become used to revealing extremely well-hidden causes of death. Many a time during autopsies an unexpected discovery had taken my breath away. But this time I was frightened; a chill ran down my spine. If Dr Mengele had discovered that I knew the secret of the chloroform injections, I'm sure at least ten doctors[26] from the *Politische Abteilung* would have come to the dissecting room to confirm the cause of my own death.

With the autopsy completed, I handed the corpses over to the crematorium, in accordance with my instructions, where they were to be immediately incinerated.

I only kept those organs which were, in some sense, interesting from the scientific point of view, so that Dr Mengele could examine them personally. Those that could also interest the institute in Berlin-Dahlem I was to preserve. They were then appropriately packed and sent off through the post. In order to make them reach the institute faster, the parcels were stamped: 'Urgent, contents important for the war effort.'

During my work at the camp I sent innumerable parcels to the institute at Berlin-Dahlem, in reply to which we would receive exhaustive scientific comments or further instructions. I had to set up separate files for this correspondence, which also included letters from the institute thanking Dr Mengele for sending particularly fascinating items.

I proceeded to dissect the remaining three pairs of twins and compare their internal organs. In every case I came to the conclusion that the cause of death was an injection of chloroform straight into the heart.

I also discovered that three of the four pairs of twins had different coloured eyes: one brown, the other blue. This phenomenon also occurs among non-twins, but here it was present in six out of only eight children! This was a fascinating concentration of one form of anomaly! In medical language it is termed heterochromous, which simply means of different colours. I took out the eyeballs and placed each in separate jars containing a formaldehyde solution. Each jar was clearly labelled, so that the eyeballs did not get mixed up.

Whilst examining the four pairs of twins I also discovered other abnormalities. Having pulled back the skin from around the neck I noticed a tumour the size of a hazelnut on the upper part of the sternum. When I pressed it with my tweezers, a thick pus came out. This was a very rare but medically known phenomenon.

The so called Dubois tumour is a symptom of hereditary syphilis. All eight twins had it. I cut out the tumours together with some of the healthy surrounding tissue and placed them in formaldehyde filled jars. I also discovered that two sets of twins had cavernous tuberculosis. All these observations were put down in the report, only the space for stating the cause of death was left empty.

Dr Mengele visited me in the afternoon. I told him about my findings and handed over the autopsy reports for five pairs of twins. He sat down to read them carefully. He was very interested in the heterochromous eyes, and even more so in the Dubois tumours. He instructed me to pack all the relevant samples, so that they could be sent off by post together with my reports and to state the cause of death for each child. It was not important to him what I wrote, provided the stated causes of death differed from one another. Almost as if trying to justify himself, he added that, as I could see for myself, the children had already been infected with syphilis and tuberculosis, so... He stopped. He'd already said enough: he had justified the murder of ten children. I didn't comment the fact in anyway. I only took note of the fact that doctors at Auschwitz did not treat tuberculosis with the artificial pneumothorax or syphilis with neosalvarsan but with lethal injections of chloroform into the heart.

It literally made my hair stand on end when I thought of how much I had learnt during my short stay at the crematorium and how much more I would have to learn, without a word of objection, before it was my turn. I realised the inevitable the moment I passed through the crematorium gate, but now that I knew so many secrets I had not the slightest doubt that I was already a dead man. It was impossible to hope that Dr Mengele and the institute at Berlin-Dahlem would ever let me leave that place alive.

IX

It was early evening. Mengele had gone. I was left alone with my dark thoughts. I went through the motions of tidying the dissecting room; I put all the instruments back in their places, washed my hands and retired to the surgery. Having just lit a cigarette and settled in a chair in order to calm down a little, I suddenly heard a terrifying scream that sent chills down my spine. Soon afterwards it was abruptly interrupted by a gunshot and then the heavy thud of a body hitting the ground. Less than a minute later there was another terrifying scream, followed by another pistol shot and the sound of a body collapsing on the floor. I counted seventy such horrifying mortal cries, seventy shots and seventy falls. Heavy footsteps faded into the distance and then all was once again quiet.

The room where this tragedy had just taken place was right next to the dissecting room with its own separate door out in the corridor. A dark, empty room with a concrete floor and a barred window looking out into the courtyard. Corpses were kept there before they were due to be dissected, and afterwards they were left there again before cremation. At the entrance to this room there was now a pile of dirty dresses, worn-down clogs, spectacles and dried up pieces of bread: all the characteristic personal items of women concentration camp inmates.

I entered the room. After what I had heard I braced myself to see something shocking, but the scene I now encountered, as I looked round the darkened room, surpassed all my imaginings of gruesomeness. Before me lay seventy naked, bloody bodies of young women. Piled one on top of the other, drenched in blood. I came up closer. The horror mounted as I gradually realised that not all of them were yet dead. The arms and legs of some were moving about in convulsions; they raised their bloody heads, their eyes were wide open.

I lifted one of the moving heads, then another, and another and discovered a further truth: apart from gassings and lethal injections, there was a third method of killing people at Auschwitz. A shot in the back of the head. The size of the hole where the bullet had entered the head told me that it had been fired from a so called small calibre, six-millimetre, gun. There was no wound or other sign of the bullet leaving the head. This would suggest that a soft lead bullet was used: the skull would flatten it out and it would stay inside the head. Unfortunately I was a professional who within a few moments could establish the precise cause of death. Despite the scorch marks on the skin which indicated that the shots had been fired from a distance of some two or three centimetres straight into the occiput, I now understood why some of the women were not yet dead. If the bullet missed by one or two millimetres, it did not cause immediate death.

This, too, I made a mental note of, but I didn't want to think anymore for fear that I might lose my mind. I went out into the courtyard and asked one of the *Sonderkommando* members where the seventy unfortunate women had come from. 'They were selected from camp C [BIIc],' he replied. 'Every evening at seven a lorry delivers seventy victims. They all receive a shot in the back of the head.'

With a heavy head, feeling dazed, I walked down the gravelled pathways and green lawns, and observed the evening chores of the *Sonderkommando*. There was no night shift that day: Crematorium I was not working. I looked across at crematoria II, III and VI. There the chimneys were blazing as usual.

It was still too early for supper. The *Sonderkommando* had brought out a football and two teams were being formed: the SS versus the *Sonderkommando*. The warders took up their positions on one side of the pitch, as did the Sonderkommando prisoners on the other. And soon the ball was in play. Loud laughter rang out in the courtyard. The spectators, also made up of members of the SS and *Sonderkommando*, enthusiastically supported their particular teams and egged the players on as if this were an ordinary football game in a small town. In silent amazement I also made note of this, but did not wait for the match to finish, and instead retired to my room. After supper I swallowed two 0.1 g tablets of luminal. I was on the verge of a nervous breakdown and all I wanted to do was sleep, to fall into deep, luminal induced slumber – that was my only escape.

X

I woke up in the morning feeling a bit groggy. I went to the shower room next door and stood for half an hour beneath a torrent of ice-cold water. I felt that it had a beneficial effect on my frayed nerves. It also revived me from my luminal induced hangover. Once again I encountered the German sense of order: the *Sonderkommando* has been provided with a shower room for ten people with white tiles. They were obliged to take a shower twice a day. This was an obligation everyone was happy to fulfil.

I was now ready to take my elegant medical bag. One of the *Sonderkommando* prisoners had brought it to me from the undressing room, where it had been left by a doctor who was sentenced to die in the gas chamber. The bag contained equipment for measuring blood pressure, a stethoscope, syringes, various instruments and ampoules for first aid injections. All this was extremely useful for my visits, which included all four crematoria. They began with the building where I lived. I started by visiting patients in the SS quarters. There were always patients there: everyone wanted to take three or four days sick leave in order get some respite from their exhausting work. However, there were occasionally some more serious cases.

Treating patients was not a problem. As far as medical supplies were concerned, we could compete with the best pharmacies in Berlin. This was because of a special *Kommando* whose job it was to open and search all the luggage and parcels brought in by transports destined for the gas chamber. The prisoners were instructed to carefully gather all the medicines and hand them over to me. It was then my job to sort them out. This wasn't easy because the transports came in from all over Europe and the medicines were labelled in various languages. I had difficulty with deciphering the Greek, Polish, Czech and Dutch labels. It was characteristic that most of the medicines found on the transports were sedatives and tranquillisers – the was symptomatic of the nervous state of European inhabitants who were gradually being driven to death.

Having finished my visit of the SS patients, I went to the *Sonderkommando* quarters. Here I had treat several burns wounds. This was a frequent complaint among prisoners working at the crematorium ovens. Members of the *Sonderkommando* rarely suffered from organic diseases. Their clothes and bedding were clean, their food was good, one could even say excellent. Besides, they had all been selected for this *Kommando* because they were young, strong and healthy. On the other hand, these people were more susceptible psychological problems. Knowledge of the terrible truth that this was where their brothers, wives, children, parents and countless kinsmen had been murdered, where every day thousands of bodies were dragged on the concrete floor and incinerated, that they themselves were gradually being turned into dust, all this caused severe depression and melancholy. Everyone of them had had a very painful past and a future they could only dread, for each *Sonderkommando* had a very limited life span. The tragic experiences of the camp's four-year history told them that no *Sonderkommando* lasted for much longer than four months. After that came the day when a larger unit of SS-men unexpectedly appeared, rounded up the *Sonderkommando* prisoners in the crematorium backyard, then a sudden hail of bullets and it was over. Half an hour later another, newly selected *Sonderkommando* would arrive[27]. They would undress their dead predecessors, of whom, half an our later, only a handful of ash remained. The first task of the new *Kommando* was to burn the bodies of the previous one.

Every time I visited the *Sonderkommando* quarters there were those would take me to one side and confidentially ask me for a poison that killed swiftly and effectively. I always refused. Today I regret it. It would have been better for them to die quickly, as and when they wanted to. They wanted to kill themselves, instead they were murdered by their oppressors.

XI

The next stage of my round was Crematorium II. It was separated from Crematorium I by a field and the railway track leading to the Jewish ramp. Both buildings had been built according to the same design. They had identical undressing rooms, gas chambers, crematorium ovens, SS and *Sonderkommando* sleeping quarters. The only difference was that the area where the dissecting room and surgery were situated in Crematorium I served in Crematorium II as a small gold smelting plant. It was the place where all the gold teeth, jewellery, gold coins, precious stones, platinum, watches, cigarette cases and other objects made of precious metals that were collected from the transports or extracted from corpses ended up. Three master goldsmiths worked there. First they disinfected the booty and then they proceeded to segregate it. They extracted the precious stones from their settings before the gold was put into the smelting pot. The daily 'output' from all the gold teeth and other valuable items was 30-35 kilograms of gold ingots.

The smelted gold was poured into graphite moulds to form disks approximately five centimetres in diameter. Each disk weighed 140 grams. I know this as a fact because I weighed one on the scales in my laboratory.

However, the gold teeth extracted from the corpses lying in front of the ovens were not all thrown into the buckets filled with hydrochloric acid. Some of them, in larger or smaller quantities, ended up in the dentists' pockets. It all depended on how close the SS guards were standing. The same thing was done by the *Kom-*

mando employed to search for gold coins, precious stones and other valuables in the luggage and clothes of the gas chamber victims. This was an extremely dangerous, life threatening thing to do, for the SS guards were everywhere and kept a close eye on all valuables expropriated by the Third Reich, especially gold and precious stones.

Initially I had my doubts as to whether the appropriation of gold by the *Sonderkommando* was moral. After several days, however, once I was more orientated in the situation, I realised that this conduct was justified.

Sonderkommando prisoners also took the gold they had hidden from the SS to the smelting plant. Despite the tight security, there were ways of smuggling it in. The prisoners later got the gold back in the form of 140-gram disks. It was a far more difficult matter to sell or rather exchange the gold for necessary items. Obviously no one there thought of saving this gold, for everyone was aware of the fact that within four months they'd be dead. In such a situation four months was an incredibly long time. In those four months one wanted to make life as easy and bearable as possible. And this was where gold became useful.

Already at the time of the first *Sonderkommando* the 140--gram gold disk became an unofficial currency. There were no smaller moulds at the smelting unit, so there were no smaller disks. The market prices of the outside world were quite irrelevant in this case. Those who sold the gold had already lost their lives once they had passed through the crematorium gate, whereas those who took the gold in exchange for goods were putting their lives on the line twice: once when they smuggled the gold out of the camp and past the SS security cordons, and then again when they smuggled goods back into the camp – goods which were also very difficult to acquire on the outside, since almost everything was rationed. Both sides risked being searched. The gold began its journey in the pocket of a *Sonderkommando* prisoner who approached the crematorium gate and exchanged a few words with the SS on guard duty there. The SS-man would then turn around and move away from the gate. At the same time there would be a group of some 20-25 Polish railway workers and their foreman working near crematorium perimeter. The *Sonderkommando* prisoner would then give the sign and one of the railwaymen would hand over a folded sack in exchange for the gold ingot, which was always wrapped in paper. Thus the sack would make its way into the camp and the railwaymen would take not only the gold but also the next day's order.

The *Sonderkommando* prisoner would then go to the guardhouse next to the gate and produce from the sack 100 cigarettes and a bottle of vodka. The SS-man would quickly hide the bottle and cigarettes in his pockets. He would be happy because SS guards got just two cigarettes a day and vodka only on special occasions. And such items were especially precious at the crematorium as a means of obviating the senses. Both the SS and the Sonderkommando were heavy drinkers and smokers.

Other goods to reach the camp in this way included mainly butter, ham, onions and eggs, because the transports didn't deliver such food. The prisoners' gold was acquired collectively and so the proceeds also went to everyone involved. The crematorium commander and all the SS non-commissioned officers also received a considerable share in the form of cigarettes, alcohol and food. Of course, everyone pretended to know nothing, because they didn't want to know anything; it was just more convenient and profitable for them that way. Individually, every SS-man at the crematorium could be won over. They were only scared of their colleagues finding out. However, they knew that no one in the *Sonderkommando* would betray them. Therefore all bribes and transactions were carried out on a one to one basis. Every SS-man received his own, individual share.

Another item to be smuggled into the crematorium every day was the *Völkischer Beobachter*, the daily for Third Reich officials. It was delivered by the railway workers' foreman. The monthly subscription fee was one 140-gram ingot of gold. A reward fully deserved by someone who for thirty days dared to deliver newspapers to a concentration camp prisoner. Since my arrival at the crematorium I had also been receiving this daily. I read it in safe seclusion and then related the latest news to the *Kommando's Schreiber* (clerk). He in turn told his colleagues and within a few hours everyone was fully informed of the most recent developments.

The *Sonderkommando* lived in bright, clean, spacious quarters. They slept on soft pillows beneath warm quilts; they had excellent food and wore elegant clothes. They had cigarettes and alcohol. Perhaps that was the reason why inter-personal relationships at the crematorium never became so brutalised as in the camp cubicles, where hungry, louse infested inmates would be at each other's throats for the sake of a piece of bread or half a potato. The conduct of the *Sonderkommando* members was genuinely decent. The rule was to help others whenever possible. For several days 500 women prisoners were building a road outside the gate, watched over by two SS-men with guard dogs. The women had to carry stones to the road. Having gained unofficial permission from their own guards, some of the *Sonderkommando* prisoners establish contact with the two SS-men in charge of the women and handed each of them a box of cigarettes. The matter was settled. Three or four of the women carrying stones came closer to the gate and pretended to be working there. In an instant they took the sweaters, shoes and underwear that had already been prepared for them. They also got cigarettes, bacon and bread. The women took turns to approach the gate and the Sonderkommando prisoners also took turns to casually approach the gate, close enough to hand them their gifts. This was purely a matter of honour. None of the *Sonderkommando* members knew any of the women prisoners, and yet they gave them hundreds of items of clothing, stockings, jumpers, cigarettes and soap. And the women walked happy. The next day the procedure was repeated. The crematorium storerooms were exceedingly well stocked.

The *Sonderkommando* helped thousands of people. I also made a contribution. I would stuff my pockets with vitamin pills, sulfamidic powder for wounds, bandages and small bottles of iodine. I would return to my room three or four times in order to refill my pockets with these invaluable, life-giving medicaments and then give them to those who needed them so very much.

After Crematorium II, I visited Crematoria III and IV. Apart from Poles and Greeks, there were also a hundred Hungarian deportees employed in the *Sonderkommando* of Crematorium III. The *Sonderkommando* at Crematorium IV, however, was made up mainly of Poles and Frenchmen[28].

I saw work proceeding apace everywhere. The Jewish ramp was like a turbulent river constantly spewing out new victims bound for the gas chamber. Appalled, I observed how the individual elements worked harmoniously together in this colossal death factory, the cleverly devised mechanics of the whole operation, the diabolical organisation of work in hell. It seemed as if it had all been established for eternity. Conjecturing that for some miraculous reason I were ever to be set free and at liberty to tell others what I had seen, I was convinced no would believe me. No words were able to express what was happening around me. Nonetheless, I did try to preserve the image in my mind, so that I would never forget.

XII

I had acquired a 'Petit Larousse' encyclopaedia with maps where I could look up the places I read about in the newspapers. One day I was referring to these maps to study the situation on the Western, Southern and Eastern fronts when suddenly I heard footsteps approaching my room. Having immediately turned the pages to hide the maps, I glanced apprehensively at the door. My visitor turned out to be the crematorium commander, who informed me that the dissecting room had to be made ready, because at two that afternoon a large commission would be paying a visit.

The first to pull up was the hearse; a shiny black limousine bearing the body of a *Haupsturmführer SS*. The corpse was placed on the dissecting table as it had arrived: in an SS uniform.

The commission arrived exactly on time. It was made up of high-ranking, elegantly dressed SS officers including: a physician of the rank of *Standartenführer*, a state prosecutor, an examining judge, two Gestapo investigating officers and a court-martial clerk. A few minutes later Doctor Mengele arrived and asked the visitors to sit down. They began conferring among themselves. The investigating officers proceeded to relate how the body had been found. The bullet wounds indicated that this was an assassination or another type of murder. The dead man's pistol was still in its holster on his belt, which ruled out suicide. We could conjecture that the perpetrator had been one of the victim's former colleagues or possible someone else who had had a grudge against him. Assassination, however, seemed to be the most likely explanation – many Poles lived in Gliwice and the surrounding areas, which meant that partisan activity and assassinations were common.

The dissection was supposed to establish whether the victim

was shot from the front or from behind as well as the calibre of the gun and the range from which it was fired. It was to be performed at the crematorium because there was no coroner in Gliwice at the time. Being only 40 kilometres from Gliwice, Auschwitz was therefore the nearest appropriate utility.

I had never even imagined that I, a Jewish concentration camp prisoner, would ever be allowed to 'sully' the body of a deceased SS officer with my hands, let alone dissect it! When I was still a free man a law was introduced prohibiting among other things Jewish physicians from treating Catholics and Aryans.

I was therefore very surprised when Dr Mengele told me to carry out the autopsy. First one had to undress the corpse, which was not an easy thing to do. Pulling off knee boots was a particularly arduous task requiring two people, so I asked for permission to have an assistant. The commission members observed our work and conferred heatedly among themselves, and paid hardly any attention to me and my helpers.

I carried out the first incisions with some trepidation. Nonetheless, I used swift, skilful movements to cut the scalp and pull one half of the skin over the face and the other round the back of the neck. The next stage was trickier: sawing off and removing the top of the skull. Nonetheless I also performed this task quickly and in textbook fashion. Now it was time to examine both wounds. If a bullet goes right through a body, there naturally have to be two wounds: at the point of entry and at the point of exit. In most cases it is easy for a professional to distinguish the entry point from the exit point as the wound of the former is usually smaller than that of the latter. Here, however, a chest wound just beneath the left nipple and another wound on the upper part of the left shoulder blade were of identical size.

This case was far from a clear-cut and therefore interesting. How could one account for identical entry and exit wounds? One had to find an explanation for facts that contradicted experience.

Suddenly Dr Mengele came up with a hypothesis that the wounds could have not been made by one bullet travelling straight through the body, but by two bullets entering the body and not coming out. Perhaps the victim had been first shot in the chest and then, after he had fallen, shot again, in the back. This line of reasoning made sense, so it needed to be checked. I began by following the path of the bullet hole in the chest. I was able to establish that the bullet had gone through the heart and then grazed the left side of the spinal column to travel upwards at a 35° angle and reach the upper part of the left shoulder blade. It broke off a piece of the shoulder blade before leaving the body. The situation was now clear. We were dealing with the damage caused by only one bullet: all the evidence suggested that it was fired from the front because its path rose at a 35° angle from the chest to the back. The entry and exit wounds appeared to be identical because the bullet had lost a lot of momentum before leaving the body by grazing the spine and breaking the shoulder blade. No one would have chosen to fire downwards at a 35° angle: in order to do this, one would have had to raise one's arm high up in the air, which would have been very conspicuous. Partisans did not shoot people that way. They didn't have to; they could fire their guns level. The gun that had killed the *Haupsturmführer* could not have been fired from the back but from the front, at close quarters, from a revolver pointed upwards. Who had fired it? Was it a stranger or someone the *Haupsturmführer* had known? Those were questions for the German police to answer.

I could see that the commission members were pleased with my work. Moreover, they announced that they would be sending all cases requiring autopsies here in the future. They decided that this was the most convenient and best solution. Thus after carrying out a successful autopsy, I, a concentration camp prisoner cum physician became simultaneously coroner for the Gliwice district. Most probably no one else in the world held a similar post!

XIII

One day in the early afternoon I received instructions over the phone to report immediately at Brzezinka, the place where the pyres were. I was to collect some medicines and glasses so that they could be sorted out at Crematorium I and then sent on to the Reich.

The pyres, hidden from view behind a small birch woods and surrounded by pine trees, were located some five to six hundred metres from Crematorium IV, beyond the camp's barbed wire perimeter, that is, between the small and large *Postenkettes*[29].

This was outside the area where I had freedom of movement, so I asked for some written authorisation. I received a pass for three prisoners, for I needed two assistants to help carry the parcels. We set off in the direction of the thick, black, swirling pall of smoke. Everyone who had the misfortune to be in Auschwitz saw this billowing smoke. It was immediately noticed by those who had just disembarked the train and were lining up for selection. It was visible from every part of the camp, both day and night. In the daytime it appeared as a thick cloud over the birch woods; at night the fires in the ditches illuminated the area with an infernal glow.

We passed the crematorium. I showed the document to the SS-guard at the gate and he let through without more ado on to the open road. The meadow of fresh, green grass initially seemed serene, but I soon noticed a chain of people some one hundred metres on, some standing, others sitting beside their machineguns – and their Alsatian guard dogs.

We cut across the meadow towards the coniferous trees. Yet another barbed wire enclosure and a wooden gate, above which was a sign like the one at the crematorium: 'Access strictly prohibited to all aliens and unauthorised SS personnel.' They let us through without our even having to show the pass because we were from the *Sonderkommando*. There were sixty members of the *Sonderkommando*'s dayshift already working there. They worked from seven in the morning to seven in the evening, then they were replaced by the nightshift, a sixty-prisoner *Kommando* from Crematorium IV.

Through the gate we entered a kind of courtyard, in the centre of which stood a building with a straw roof and flaying white-wash. Shutters covered its small windows. A rural hut[30], or at least that is what it had been for the previous 150 years, judging by its roof darkened with age and the thick layers of plaster. The hamlet of Brzezinka (Birkenau) used to lie close to Oświęcim (Auschwitz) until the Germans built their camp there. Then all the inhabitants were evicted and their dwellings, with the exception of this hut, demolished. What had been the initial purpose of this building? Did people ever live there? Now that the partition walls had been removed it was just one large chamber adapted for a specific function. Or perhaps it had always been like this? Perhaps it had initially been some kind of a storehouse? I couldn't tell, but now it served as an undressing room – those who were about to die on the pyre left their clothes there.

When all four crematoria were working to capacity, new transports arriving at the Jewish ramp were directed to this birch wood, where the worst possible death awaited them. Unlike the other prisoners they didn't even get quench their thirst with water. There were no notices to temporarily delude them. There was no building they could mistake for a bathhouse. There was only the hut with a straw roof and onetime white plaster; a peasant's hovel with shuttered windows, and behind it a huge column of smoke and all around the smell of burning human flesh and smouldering human hair.

In the courtyard stood a throng of about five thousand terrified people. They were surrounded by a dense line of SS-men with large Alsatians straining at their leashes. Three to four hundred victims entered the hut at a time. Driven on with incessant truncheon blows, they were made to take off all their clothes and leave through an exit at the opposite end of the hut. Outside they didn't even have time to take in the horror of what was going on around them, for two members of the *Sonderkommando* grabbed each prisoner by the arm from either side and led them in between two lines of SS-men, down a winding pathway through the clump of pine trees. They only saw the pyre once they had reached the end of this path and come out into a clearing.

The pyre was a ditch 50 metres long, 6 metres wide, and 3 metres deep containing hundreds of burning bodies. Each pyre was surrounded by SS-men holding special six-millimetre guns for shooting in the back of the head. The moment the unfortunate victim emerged from behind the trees, he or she was seized by another two *Sonderkommando* men and dragged some 15 to 20 metres to end up before the barrel of an SS-man's gun. Even the crack of the pistol shot was drowned out by the ghastly screams of dying people. The bullet fired from a small-calibre pistol was usually insufficient to kill the victim, who was then cast into the inferno still alive[31].

The overall commander of the crematoria and pyres was *Oberscharführer* Moll[32]. As a doctor and eyewitness, I can testify that this was the most callous and depraved criminal of the Third Reich. In comparison to Moll, one could even find some semblance of human feelings in Mengele. There were very rare occasions, when during a selection on the Jewish ramp, young, good-looking women would defy orders and join their mothers in the left column. It was then that Mengele, using coarse language, would order them to rejoin the right column. Even the chief executioner of Crematorium 1, *Oberscharführer* Muhsfeldt, would occasionally shoot a second time if his victim did not die instantly.

Oberscharführer Moll, on the other hand, had no time for such gestures.

Moll was everywhere, tirelessly circling the pyre and prowling the path between the building and the fire hundreds of times. Most people allowed themselves to be led to their place of execution without putting up any resistance. Fear paralysed them to such an extent that they might not even have been aware of what was about to happen to them. That seemed to be particularly the case with the children and the very old. The instinct of self preservation, however, drove some of the young people to put up a struggle. Whenever Moll spotted such a scene unfolding somewhere in the midst of the human procession, he would instantly pull out his pistol from its holster, which is always left open, and fire from a distance of say 40 or 50 metres. The struggling prisoner dropped dead instantly, for Moll was a crack marksman. He also had the habit of shooting holes through the hands of *Sonderkommando* prisoners when he was dissatisfied with their work. He would always hit just the hand, and do so without calling or giving any other warning signs.

I collected the spectacles and medicines that had been left for me. Traumatised, on trembling legs, we headed 'home' to Crematorium I, which as Doctor Mengele put it, was not a sanatorium but quite bearable. He was right. After what I had seen that day, I knew he exactly what he meant.

On my return I went straight to my room. I was in no state to sort out the medicines and spectacles that day. I took some luminal and went straight to bed. This time the dose was 0.3g., but I still wasn't sure whether it would be enough to help me overcome the sickness brought on by the spectre of the pyres.

XIV

I woke up. A new day – new experiences. Inside the camp every day had its terrible moments, so terrible that I could never have previously imagined them.

This day those members of the *Sonderkommando* who were always the best informed told us that nobody was allowed to leave their barracks. SS soldiers were patrolling the streets and alleys in between the blocks and had let their Alsatian guard dogs off their leashes. Today was the day they were liquidating the Czech camp.

There were originally 15,000 prisoners at the Czech camp who had been transported from the ghetto in Terezin. As in the Gypsy camp, here too families were initially allowed to live together. They also did not undergo a 'selection' on arrival. Conditions were very hard, but at least the old, young and very young could be together. Czech Jews wore their own clothes and were not forced to work. That was how they had lived until now. For now their hour had come. After all, the camp at Auschwitz was a death camp! Sooner or later all its inmates were to be annihilated.

Transports of Jews from Hungary were arriving one after the other. Frequently two trains arrived at once. On such occasions people literally poured out of the boxcars like a river. What Dr Mengele did on the ramp now could longer be called selection. His hand was pointing in only one direction: to the left! Entire transports were immediately sent to either the gas chambers or the blazing ditches. Although transports were also departing every day for other camps, the Auschwitz quarantine camp, C [BIIc] camp, D [BIId] camp as well as FKL[33] were all filled to maximum capacity. The old, the infirm and drastically emaciated children had to make room for the newly arrived who were still fit enough to work.

The order to confine all prisoners to barracks came in the early morning. Several SS companies surrounded the Czech camp and drove the inmates out to roll call. There was terrible screaming when those awaiting death were loaded onto the lorries. They were fully aware of what was going to happen to them; they had after all been in the camp for more than long enough to know. On this final day there were 12,000 people in the Czech camp[34]. One and a half thousand men and women including eight physicians were selected for work. The rest were sent to crematoria II and III.

The next day the Czech camp was empty. The manic work at crematoria II and III was also over. All I saw was a lorry loaded with ash leaving the crematorium and turning towards the Vistula.

The camp's population was suddenly reduced by 10,000 human beings, yet the camp's archives were increased by only one document. The official form contained a short note: 'Owing to an outbreak of typhus which was concentrated in the so called Czech section of Auschwitz concentration camp, the said subsidiary camp was liquidated.' It was signed: 'Dr Mengele, *Haupstsurmführer, Lagerarzt.*'

Dr Mengele spared the lives of the eight physicians from the Czech camp thanks to the intervention of Dr Epstein[35]. By then these doctors, having in recent days dedicated all their energies to fighting a real typhus epidemic and caring for the sick, were both physically and mentally exhausted. They also contracted typhus and ended up in hospital at camp section F [BIIf]. It so happened that the day the Czech camp was liquidated I was on official business in that particular section and thus able to talk with the world-famous Doctor Heller from Prague, who was chief physician for the prisoners of the Czech camp. He told me about the sufferings and extermination of Czechoslovakia's Jewish intelligentsia[36].

Soon these eight brave physicians were also dead. They were real doctors. They deserve to be remembered with the deepest esteem.

XV

Close to the former Czech camp there was the C camp [BIIc] where Jewish women from Hungary were incarcerated. Although transports had been departing for other camps every day, the population in this section sometimes reached 60,000. Then, one day physicians diagnosed some cases of scarlet fever in this overpopulated camp. On Mengele's order, a strict quarantine was imposed on the prisoners of the barracks where the disease's symptoms had been identified as well as those of the two neighbouring barracks. The quarantine lasted from early morning until the evening, when lorries took the inhabitants of all three barracks to the crematorium. Such were the measures Dr Mengele resorted to in an attempt to effectively check the outbreak of an epidemic.

Dr Mengele's actions to combat epidemics had already resulted in the extermination of the Czech camp and three barracks in section C [BIIc]. Fortunately the physicians immediately realised how the process worked and made sure not to inform the SS health authorities of any further cases of infectious diseases. Sick prisoners were kept hidden from view in the darkest, farthest cubicle of the barracks and treated with medicines from what meagre supplies there were. They were no longer sent to the camp hospital, where SS doctors did the rounds. The latter had no time subtleties; the discovery of an infected prisoner resulted in the liquidation of not only the barracks the patient came from but also the blocks on either side. In SS language this was called 'broad preventive action against the outbreak of an epidemic'. The outcome of such an action was two or three lorry loads of ash.

70

I had used similar terminology when I was myself a doctor dealing with sanitary conditions and epidemics. In practice, however, I would combat the spreading of diseases by isolating patients infected with, say, diphtheria or typhus from other people and vaccinating the inhabitants of neighbouring houses. But this was now another place, another code of conduct.

Some time shortly after the aforementioned incidents at Auschwitz the bodies of two women were brought to the crematorium along with instructions from Dr Mengele for me to perform autopsies. As always, I began by carefully reading the two dead women's medical records. In both cases the diagnosis findings indicated typhoid and the stated cause of death was heart failure. There were question marks next to all these entries. I am not one usually given to pause and weigh the pro and con before acting. I decide quickly and act quickly, especially when it is a question of an important decision. The results are not always brilliant. The fact that I had ended up here in the crematoriums was the result of a snap decision.

I immediately decided that the autopsy findings Dr Mengele received would not confirm the diagnosis of typhoid. I just would not let it happen. Besides, the description of the symptoms was incomplete and the identification of the disease therefore open to question. Dr Mengele did not yet know for sure what the disease was, otherwise he would not have sent me the two bodies. That was the sole purpose of the whole post-mortem examination.

Having proceeded with the dissection, I found that in both cases the small intestine had all the symptoms of the later stages of typhoid: they both had typical typhoid ulceration that was at least three weeks old. Also in both cases the spleen was swollen. This was typhoid beyond all doubt!

Dr Mengele arrived, as usual, at around five. As he approached me his face was so cheerful that it seemed almost implausible to associate the man with such unspeakable cruelty. He enquired about my findings with apparent interest. The opened up corpses lay on the table. The dissected large and small intestines as well as the spleens lay in separate bowls, so that they too could be inspected if the doctor so wished. My official diagnosis was colitis of the small intestine with extensive ulceration. I gave Dr Mengele a virtual lecture on the difference between three-week-old typhoid ulceration and ulcers resulting from colitis. I also proved to him that the swelling of the spleen was a frequent symptom of colitis of the intestines. Therefore the ailment was not typhoid but colitis of the small intestine with heavy ulceration, most probably the result of food poisoning.

Doctor Mengele was a specialist of racial biology not forensic medicine. I therefore had no difficulty in convincing him that my diagnosis was correct. However, he was clearly angered by the implication that the earlier diagnosis had been wrong. He expressed this by declaring that the women-prisoner physicians who had made such a serious mistake should carry stones rather than work in the camp hospital. Their error had cost the lives of patients who could have otherwise been saved.

He took the autopsy reports, but wrote something down in the margin before putting them into his briefcase. Standing behind him, I could see by glancing over his shoulder the words 'Rücksprache m. Ärztinnen' – in rough translation it simply means that both physicians are to be held responsible.

I deeply regretted having exposed fellow prisoners to the threat of punishment for what was in fact a perfectly accurate diagnosis. Now they would most probably lose their jobs and end up in the road-building Kommando, where they'd be forced to do hard labour. It would be my fault if Dr Mengele fulfilled the written resolution.

I admit that I broke the medical code of conduct, but within that barbed wire enclosure different medical ethics applied. My fictitious report got two or three people into trouble; but how 'broad' would Dr Mengele's 'preventive action against the outbreak of an epidemic' have been had I proceeded otherwise?

The next day I was relieved to find out that Dr Mengele had merely berated the two women physicians and they suffered no further consequences. They kept their jobs at the hospital.

I was later to receive many more prisoner corpses and many more cards with medical histories, but the spaces for diagnosis were never again filled. I also never again made any entries there, they were best kept empty. How cynical was Dr Mengele's indignation because of an apparent mistake in diagnosis that had cost the lives of two patients! The notion of such cynicism preyed on my mind for several days. It was the cynicism of a criminal!

XVI

One afternoon I received instructions to immediately report to Dr Mengele at the *Schreibstube* of section F [BIIf]. I was happy to fulfil this command, for at least it allowed me to escape for a few hours from the depressing atmosphere of the crematorium. Besides, the walk wouldn't do me any harm either. After the odours of the dissecting room and crematorium it would be good to catch a breath of fresh air. I was also happy to be afforded the opportunity of talking with the doctors of section F [BIIf], who had been so kind and friendly towards me during my first days at the camp.

I prepared for my trip by stuffing my pockets with precious medicines and also taking several packets of cigarettes. I couldn't revisit the barracks where I had first stayed at the camp empty-handed. It would not have been befitting of a worker of the *Sonderkommando*.

Having let the guard take down my camp number, I passed through the iron gate of the crematorium enclosure and headed for section F [BIIf]. I was in no hurry and tried to make the most of the short walk. Passing the barbed-wire enclosure of the women's camp, I saw thousands of female prisoners milling around the barracks. They all looked alike with their shaven heads and rags instead of clothes. I thought of my wife and my fifteen-year-old daughter, of her plush long hair. I suddenly remembered all her dresses, whose styles we would jointly conjure up during our evenings together as a family.

Three months had passed since we were separated on the ramp. What had happened to them? Were they still together? Were they still in one of the women's camps at Auschwitz? Or had they perhaps been sent to another camp somewhere in the Third Reich. Three months was a long time. In a concentration camp it was virtually an eternity! Despite everything, I felt they were still somewhere the camp, but where? Which of the numerous barbed-wire fences separated us? Wherever I looked, everywhere, right up to the horizon, I saw rows of concrete posts, barbed wire and warning signs. The whole concentration camp was a intricate web of barbed wire.

I reached section F [BIIf]. At the gate there was a *Blockführerstube*, the guardhouse. On duty was a dense-looking SS non-commissioned officer and a private. In accordance with camp regulations, I approached the small window of the guardhouse, pulled up my coat sleeve and read out my camp number: A 8450. In so doing I also revealed my wristwatch. The possession and wearing of watches was a very serious offence in a concentration camp, but I had Dr Mengele's permission to wear one on account of my work. The SS non-commissioned officer leapt out of the *Blockführerstube* like a tiger. Yelling at me in a hoarse voice, he demanded to know my business in section F [BIIf] and the reason why I was wearing a wristwatch. Three months at the crematorium, however, had prepared me well for such situations. I stayed put, without even flinching, looked straight into his eyes and replied that I had come on Dr Mengele's orders. I added that Dr Mengele wanted to speak to me personally but if I were not allowed to enter the camp, I would return to the crematorium and report to him over the telephone.

The name Mengele worked like magic. Everyone feared him. The SS-man immediately changed his tone and enquired, now very politely, how long I intended to stay in the section, explaining that he had to record it in the register. I looked at my watch, which no longer caused any offence: it was ten o'clock. I decided to stay till two in the afternoon, which I assumed to be enough for whatever business Dr Mengele had with me. Saying this, I pulled out a packet of twenty cigarettes and handed a few of them to the SS-man, so that he had something smoke until my return. He was pleased to receive them. We now parted company on quite friendly terms, the German almost implying that he would be more than happy to see me in the future. My boss's name and the cigarettes having proved their worth, I could now look forward to spending an hour or two with my colleagues. First, however, I had to report to Dr Mengele.

I entered the barracks and waited in the lobby until the clerk on duty asked me my business. He pointed to one of the doors. On entering the room I found myself in a nicely furnished surgery. Numerous charts and graphs illustrating the camp population over various periods of time covered the walls. On another wall hung an ornately framed portrait of Himmler. There were three other men in the room: Dr Mengele; *Haupsturmführer* Thilo MD[37], the chief surgeon; and *Obersturmführer* Wolff MD, who was in charge of the camp's department of internal diseases. Dr Mengele introduced me to Dr Wolff and informed him that I was the autopsy specialist working at the crematorium. The latter then turned to me and said that he was very interested in post-mortems and would have visited the crematorium a long time ago to observe a particularly interesting dissection were he not so busy. Currently, however, he had undertaken a major scientific work and I had been summoned because he wished to discuss the matter with me. There was an increasing number of prisoners suffering from diarrhoea in the camp and in 90 percent of the cases this condition proved fatal. The doctor had absolutely no doubts as to the course of the disease from the clinical point of view; he had studied thousands of cases and collected detailed descriptions and notes. Nonetheless, his research was incomplete because such an extensive clinical study needed to be supported by post-mortem findings.

Doctor Wolff was therefore yet another 'medical scientist'. He, too, wanted to exploit the bloody concentration camp, the crematoria and study hundreds of living skeletons, humans weighing only 30 kilograms and suffering from diarrhoea, in order to make scientific discoveries. He now commanded me to dissect hundreds of dead people only because he wanted to the discoverer the disease's internal symptoms and only because they were not yet officially known in the medical world. Doctor Mengele was trying to unravel the secret of reproduction by dissecting the bodies of countless numbers of twins. Doctor Wolff, on the other hand, wanted to discover the reason why such vast numbers of people were suffering from dysentery, even though the causes of this disease were obvious.

The recipe for concentration camp dysentery was as follows: you snatched a person – man, woman or child – from their home and, having first robbed them of all their belongings and weakened them during a six-week stay in a crowded ghetto, you then packed them together with hundreds of other people into a cattle truck to be sent off all the way to Auschwitz with the only provisions being one bucket of foul water. Then this person, along with thousands of other prisoners, would be put in a barracks where conditions were unfit for a stable. Like everyone else, all they had to eat was mouldy bread, which was in fact a baked mixture of flour and sawdust, synthetic margarine and three decagrams of sausage made from the meat of a mangy horse – all together this amounted to 700 calories a day[38]. The said victim washed all this down with a soup made from nettles or swede, without any fat, salt or flour. Within four or five days they had diarrhoea. Within three or four weeks the disease would have run its course and, regardless of even the most tender medical care, our human guinea pig would inevitably die.

Doctor Wolff was of the opinion that his scientific study should be supported by the findings of 150 post-mortems. Doctor Mengele added that I was able to perform seven dissections a day, which would imply that the work could be done over a period of approximately three weeks. I was of a different opinion and argued that if – as I was convinced – they required me to do proper, scientific work, then I would only be able to perform no more than three autopsies a day. They accepted my arguments and, with a nod of the head, allowed me to leave.

I found my colleagues from the hospital in Block 12. They were very pleased to receive the medicines and the cigarettes, but as they smoked their faces looked tired and their words expressed despondency. They still hadn't got over the terrifyingly tragic liquidation of the Czech camp. What was more, they were becoming increasingly aware of the futility of their own situation. Unlike me, they hadn't given up all hope of survival; their faith was being worn away gradually, day after day. I had been spared this drawn-out process, for the moment I had passed through the crematorium gate I lost all illusions regarding my future. Despite all this, I tried to be comforting and encouraged them to persevere. I told them about the situation on the front. I read the newspaper every day and was able pass on detailed information.

We parted company after exchanging firm handshakes. Nowhere else were farewells as sincere and heartfelt as over there, in the concentration camp. Every time we said goodbye, we did not know whether we would ever meet again. Saying farewell was virtually like parting company for aeons. However, I left with a quiet air of satisfaction that I was after all a strong individual who, despite the hopelessness of his own situation, was able to raise the morale of others.

XVII

One after another, Dr Wolff's former patients who had died of dysentery came under the lancet. I had just performed the thirtieth autopsy and proceeded sum up my findings so far.

In all the cases the autopsies had revealed an inflammation of the stomach's mucous membrane resulting in the failure, or even the disappearance, of the glands producing gastric juices. Food could not be digested without these juices, instead there was increased fermentation.

My second observation was an inflammation of the mucous membrane of the small intestine and considerable thinning of the intestinal walls.

The third observation concerned the most important digestive juice of the small intestine, bile, which is essential for the digestion of fats. On opening the gall bladder a colourless sludge was revealed instead of greenish-yellow bile. This secretion in no way coloured the contents in the intestine and was therefore unable to fulfil its task in the digestive process.

The fourth observation was the inflammation of the mucous membrane in the large intestine – here too the intestinal lining was dried up, extremely thin and fragile like cigarette paper. The intestines no longer digested food they were merely conduits excreting waste. Everything that flowed in from above was expelled within minutes.

That, in general, was the sum of my findings. That was all as far as I was concerned. The bacteriological tests were carried out at the SS Institute of Hygiene and Bacteriology at Reisgau[39], which was some two or three kilometres away. The work there was supervised by a fellow prisoner, the renowned scientist Dr Mansfeld[40], a professor of Bacteriological Institute at the University of Pecs.

XVIII

My afternoon nap was interrupted by *Oberscharführer* Muhsfeldt pushing in front of him three strangers dressed in striped prisoner uniforms. Pointing at the unfortunates, he informed me that Dr Mengele had sent me some colleagues.

These poor people were in a pitiful state. They stood before me in their dirty rags, dumbstruck with fear and disoriented by the new situation they now found themselves in. They became aware of the hopelessness of their predicament the moment they passed through the crematorium gate.

We shook hands in a friendly manner and started getting to know each other. The first one I talked to was Dr Denes Görög, an anatomicopathologist from a hospital in Szombathely. A short, slim man in his mid-forties who wore thick glasses. He made a positive impression on me and I instinctively felt he'd make a good companion in this very difficult environment. The next man was around fifty, his body was hunched and stocky, and his face was unpleasant. His name was Adolf Fischer. For twenty years he had been a dissecting room assistant at the Prague Institute of Anatomy. A Czechoslovak Jew who had already been a concentration camp prisoner for four years. The third prisoner, Dr József (Jecheskiel) Körner from Nice, had been in the camp for three years. A well educated but taciturn young man, barely 32 years old.

Doctor Mengele had fished these prisoners out of the filthy barracks of section D [BIId] so that they could help me perform the autopsies faster. We divided the various tasks between us:

I would continue to be in charge of the 'scientific research', the writing of autopsy reports and all official correspondence. The two doctors would now perform the actual autopsies; while the assistant, as befitted his qualifications, would prepare the bodies for dissection, open the skulls, remove and clean those organs that needed to be examined, remove corpses that had already been dissected as well as keep the dissecting room and surgery clean and tiny.

So now I had fully qualified helpers, a fact which considerably alleviated the burden of my work. On Mengele's instructions, I was to share my room with these people. The greatest advantage of this was that at last I had companions.

XIX

I had almost ended my morning rounds. All four crematoria were working at full blast.

That night they had burnt the Greek Jews from the Mediterranean island of Corfu.[41] It was Corfu that used to have one of the oldest Jewish communities in Europe.

Their journey had lasted 27 days: first in barges across the sea, and then in boxcars, without any food or water. When the transport finally reached the Auschwitz ramp and the boxcars were opened up no one got out to line up for selection. Half of them had died on the way there, the rest were dying. The whole transport ended up in Crematorium II. The intensive work lasted all night. In the morning all that remained was a huge pile of dirty, tattered clothes in the courtyard. My heart bled when I saw these rags getting drenched in the drizzling rain.

That day I was put in a difficult situation in Crematorium IV. One of the *Sonderkommando* stokers had tried to commit suicide by taking an overdose of luminal. This was the most common form of suicide there. It was easy for *Sonderkommando* people to get hold of luminal. I approached the sick man's bed – if you could call it that – and sadly realised that it was the 'Captain'. Here he was only known by that name. Back home, in Athens, that was his army rank. He had been the tutor of the Greek king's children. An exceptionally polite and well educated man. His wife and two children had gone straight to gas chamber the very hour they arrived.

He was unconscious, lying in his bed in deep slumber. The poison he had taken a few hours earlier had already been absorbed by his metabolism. Despite this fact, his situation wasn't hopeless. The *Sonderkommando* men were all standing round his bed trying to persuade me to fulfil the Captain's wish and let him pass away. After all, he only wanted to escape from the psychological pain that he had had to endure for so long now, and besides, the twelfth *Sonderkommando* would soon be liquidated anyway. However, when they saw me calmly sterilising the hypodermic needles, they finally realised that their admonitions were having no effect on me. Then some of the older prisoners lost their temper and expressed their bitter disapproval in fairly unpleasant terms.

I left them knowing that, provided he did not subsequently contract pneumonia, the Captain would recover within four or five days. Then for a few weeks more he'd be shovelling coke into the diabolical furnace and stoking the flames that devour the bodies of thousands of fellow human beings who had been rounded up, tortured and then gassed to death. And then the day would come when he would be made to line up with other members of the *Sonderkommando*. After the fusillade he and his companions would fall to the ground in a pool of blood, the expression of horror frozen in their lifeless eyes.

Now that I am no longer at his bedside, and his suffering face no longer calls for the help which twenty years of medical experience had allowed me to provide, I admit that the Captain's companions were absolutely right. I should have let him pass away in luminal induced sleep instead of bringing him back to life only to be murdered a few weeks later.

I finished my rounds and returned to Crematorium I. My assistants were opening up the bodies of Dr Wolff's patients with the zeal of neophytes. Clean shaven, with new clothes, clean shirts and elegant shoes they had regained their human appearance. They stood at the dissecting table in their white coats, yellow rubber aprons and yellow rubber gloves. An outside observer who was unaware of what was really going on might have mistaken this for an operating theatre in a genuine scientific institute.

However, I was a professional who had been working there for three months, and was therefore fully aware that it had nothing to do with science, this was a pseudo-institute! Just like the notion of racial supremacy was pseudoscientific, as pseudoscientific as the premises on which Dr Mengele based his research into the phenomenon of twins. As wrong as the idea of using the bodies of murdered dwarfs and cripples to prove the false theory of the degeneration and inferiority of other races. The findings of these studies were by no means intended for the present generation, which would never accept them. We were working for the benefit of a future generation that was to come after the war won!

Doctor Mengele and his comrades dreamt that the skeletons of the dwarfs and cripples murdered at Auschwitz would one day stand on special pedestals with cards stating precise information – name and age – in the spacious corridors of museums. They dreamt that on anniversaries marking the victorious end of the war in defence of the German race and the millennial Third Reich's way of life school trips would come to these museums. And the teachers would celebrate this anniversary together with their pupils, and explain to them its significance. The victory would not only confirm their racial superiority by lowering the status of the French, Belgians, Russians and Poles, but also explain why one nation in Europe had to be totally annihilated, namely the Jewish nation, which despite its six thousand-year-history, had become degenerate and deformed. Moreover, this nation had threatened to contaminate the only purely Aryan race! The people had had a harmful effect on racial purity and were very dangerous because they had planned to take over the whole of Europe. That was why they had to be eliminated. It was for this reason that the first Führer of the Third Reich would become immortal and earn the admiration of the entire civilised world... That was their dream!

Those theories were the reason why they continued their war against the entire world and were even prepared to murder infants That was why in the land of National Socialism everything was false. The sea of spilled blood was called a crusade. In their eyes the whole of Russia was a wild Mongolian steppe. France was called the land of venereal disease peopled by a dying nation. According to them, the English and Scots, starting from their prime minister down, were delirious from the consumption of whisky. The Japanese, on the other hand, were regarded to be a pure Aryan race, because for the time being it was expedient to view them that way. Morality and the whole outlook on life were false there. For the sake of their race, girls, women and war widows were allowed to give themselves to any German male and bear his child which would then be given his or some other suitor's surname. They announced to the world that work not gold was the treasure of the Third Reich. Yet despite this, they had set up special installations whose purpose it was to extract gold in the most inhuman way, from victims who were brought to a camp to be murdered, all for the sake of producing a dozen or so kilograms of bullion a day. Special multilingual notices announced that the basement of the crematorium was a bathhouse, when in actual fact there were gas chambers. The label on the Zyklon tins informed us that they contain a disinfectant against cockroaches and other insects, whereas in fact it was used to kill people within seconds.

Every day every prisoner can read the sign above the concentration camp gate: '*Arbeit Macht Frei*' – freedom through work. Reality can be illustrated by the following example:

One day a train comprising three wagons pulled up along the ramp. The people who emerged from the boxcars were emaciated, barely able to stand and as yellow as lemons. There were about three hundred of them, and when they arrived at the crematorium gate I spoke with a few. They told me that three months earlier they had been sent out from section D [BIId] in a huge transport of three thousand prisoners to work in a sulphuric acid factory.

Many of their companions had died of various diseases. They themselves were suffering from sulphur poisoning, thus their yellow faces. For this reason they had been on the train that the Germans said would take them to a rest camp. Half an hour later I saw their bloody corpses lying in front of the crematorium ovens. 'Freedom through work!' 'Rest camp!'

It was either in June or July that thousands of postcards were distributed among the inmates of crowded barracks who were ordered to address them to their friends. They were also instructed to send greetings, not from Birkenau or Auschwitz but from Am Waldsee, a town on the Swiss border. The cards were posted and there was even some response. I saw with my own eyes the reply letters and postcards, some fifty thousand of them being piled up in the crematorium courtyard and burnt. There was no one they could be given to anyway: the addressees had been burnt earlier. So what was it all in aid of? The object of the exercise was to allay and mislead world public opinion.

XX

There was a pile of corpses in the gas chamber of Cremato-rium I. The *Sonderkommando* had begun to pull them down. The whirr of the lift and the sound of its slamming door reached my room. Work was proceeding at full pace. The gas chamber had to be emptied immediately, for another transport was due to arrive.

Suddenly the *Vorarbeiter* of the *Gaskommando* burst into by room and excitedly informed me that in among the corpses they had found a woman who was still alive.

I grabbed my medical bag, which was always kept at close hand, and rushed downstairs to the gas chamber. Beyond the en-trance to the vast chamber, right under the wall, partially covered by corpses, I saw the body of a young woman shaking convulsive-ly. She was wheezing loudly. The deeply concerned men of the *Gaskommando* gathered around us. Nothing like this had ever happened before.

We freed her body from beneath the corpses. I carried the light body of this young girl to the room beside gas chamber where the *Gaskommando* men changed. I laid her on one of the benches. She must have been around fifteen. I took a syringe and gave this pant-ing girl three injections, instantly, one after the other. The men co-vered her frigid body with their thick coats. Someone ran to the kitchen to fetch her some tea or soup to drink. Everyone wanted to help as if they were fighting for the life of their own child.

Our efforts at last started to have some effect. The girl had a coughing fit and expelled from her lungs a thick phlegm. Her eyes opened and stared blankly at the ceiling. I waited apprehensively for every sign of her returning to life. Her breathing was getting deeper. The lungs, debilitated by the gas, were now desperate for air. Thanks to the injections, her pulse was getting stronger. I braced myself with patience: the injections hadn't yet started working to maximum effect, but I knew that in a few minutes the girl would fully regain consciousness. And indeed she did.

The colour returned to her delicate face, her eyes now became alert. She looked at us in complete bewilderment and then closed her eyes, not yet aware of what was going on. She could not comprehend what had happened. She didn't even know if all this was real. Her perception was still hazy. She vaguely remembered the train that had brought her to where she was now. She remembered that they had made her stand in a queue, and before she knew it she was moving with the crowd. Then there was this vast, brightly lit, underground chamber. Everything was happening instantly. She remembered the order to undress. That was very unpleasant, but everyone obeyed. Naked, she was pushed with the others into another chamber. All the people had suddenly become nervous. There were huge lights in this chamber, too. She was frightened, looking for her family in the crowd, but to no avail. So she clung on to the wall and waited for what was to happen next. All at once she was plunged into darkness. Something started stinging her eyes and throat, making her choke. Then she lost consciousness. The rest was an abyss...

The girl became increasingly agitated. She raised here head and shoulders, and looked round to the left and right. Her face started having contortions. Then she grabbed me by the lapels and clinging on to them, desperately tried to sit up. I wanted to get her to lie down again, but the girl renewed her efforts with determination. This was a sharp nervous shock. She gradually stopped struggling and lay down exhausted. Huge, shiny tears welled up in her eyes, but she did not cry.

I received the first answer to a question. I didn't want to tire her, so I didn't ask too many questions; only enough to find out that she was sixteen and that she arrived with her parents on one of the Hungarian transports.

I handed her a cup of hot broth. She drank it. The men of the *Sonderkommando* had brought her various titbits, but I forbade them to give her anything. Instead I covered the girl with coats up to the neck and told her to sleep.

I was unable to collect my thoughts. Turning to my companions, together we tried to figure out what to do. The crux of the matter was what was to be done with the child. We realised that she would not be able to stay in the crematorium for long.

What chance had a little girl of surviving in a place where only the *Sonderkommando* worked! I knew the cast-iron regulation: nobody – neither the prisoners from the transports nor the *Sonderkommando* – was to leave the crematorium alive.

There was little time for consultation. *Oberscharführer* Muhsfeldt had arrived as usual to have a look round and monitor the work. Passing the open door, he immediately noticed the gathering, so he entered the room to find out what was happening. It was too late, he had already seen the girl lying there. I told the others to leave: I had decided to attempt to do the impossible on my own.

Three months spent under the same roof had shaped a very specific relationship between us. The Germans had this custom of treating with respect those who had some kind of professional knowledge that they needed, even if they happened to be concentration camp prisoners. This applied to shoemakers, tailors, carpenters and locksmiths. In my numerous encounters with Muhsfeldt I had come to the conclusion that he respected me for my expertise and the fact that I was in charge of autopsies. Moreover, Muhsfeldt knew that my boss was the camp's chief physician and one of the most feared people, Dr Mengele. With a vanity that was typical of Germans, Muhsfeldt regarded Dr Mengele to be one of the greatest luminaries of German medicine. The gassing of hundreds of thousands of people was in his eyes the fulfilment of a patriotic duty. According to him, the autopsies served the advancement of German medical knowledge! This attitude, in a way, worked to my advantage. Muhsfeldt frequently visited the dissecting room – we then usually talked about politics, the war situation and various other matters. I felt that he respected me also because he treated the dissecting of bodies as an occupation akin to his own bloody work.

Assisted by three other SS-men, Muhsfeldt was the commander and chief executioner of Crematorium I. Together they put to death selected camp inmates, as well as those from outside who had been sent to the 'rest camp'. All the victims were shot in the back of the head. This form of execution was applied when the number of victims was less than 500. The gas chamber was only used to exterminate larger numbers because the same amount of Zyklon was always required, regardless of whether it was to kill 500 or 3,000 people. Nor was it practical to send out lorries to collect the clothes or, indeed, the ambulances delivering the Zyklon and the two executioners. Out of such considerations the preferred method of murder was shooting in the back of the head.

I calmly and carefully related the girls horrific experiences. I presented to Muhsfeldt a terrifying picture of this child barely surviving death in the gas chamber. Of how everything around her had suddenly turned into darkness, and how she must have also inhaled some of the lethal Zyklon, but only a small amount, for her frail body must have been knocked over in the crowd that was by then struggling with death; and of how she must have fallen face down onto a damp patch on the concrete floor. It must have been the dampness that saved her from gas asphyxiation, for Zyklon did not work properly in moist air.

That was how I explained it to Muhsfeldt, and I then asked him to do something for the child. He treated my words seriously and asked me how I would suggest this matter to be resolved. I strongly sensed that this was a very tricky problem. The expression on his face told me that I'd put him in an awkward position. The girl obviously could not remain in the crematorium. There was only thing for it: the girl had to be taken beyond the gate. Every day there was a large women's road-building *Kommando* working close to the crematorium. In the evening the girl could return to the camp with the women, get into one of the barracks and keep her mouth shut about what had happened to her. Among so many thousands of women she would be quite inconspicuous – after all, many didn't know each other there.

'If the girl was two or three years older,' said Muhsfeldt, 'something could be done. A twenty-year-old would realise how miraculous the circumstances leading to her survival were and have enough sense not to tell anyone about her experiences. A sixteen- -year-old child, however, is naive enough to tell the first person she encounters about everything she experienced, where it happened and what she saw. The news would spread instantaneously throughout the camp. There's nothing for it,' he summed up, 'the child has to die.'

A quarter of an hour later the girl was led, or rather carried, out into the anteroom, and there she was killed with a bullet in the back of the head. The executioner wasn't Muhsfeldt: he had sent someone to replace him.

XXI

On the first floor of Crematorium I, beside the SS quarters, there was a carpenter's workshop. Three joiners were employed there. They had recently been working on a private order for *Oberscharführer* Muhsfeldt, who, taking advantage of the opportunity afforded him, commanded them to quickly make for him a huge double bed-cum-sofa. They immediately set about the task, which was by no means easy when one was limited to the crematorium premises. They had to utilise springs from armchairs that had been used to deliver the elderly and infirm on the transports – there were dozens of them in the crematorium courtyard, and we would sit in them in the evenings.

And so the bed was completed according to specifications. With my own eyes I saw it being made out odd bits of wood, cannibalised armchair springs and upholstery cut out of the finest Persian carpet. Two French electricians had fitted it with a reading lamp and a special shelf for a radio. The wooden parts of the bed had been painted bright red. It looked very grand in the crematorium loft, but it would look even more impressive in *Oberscharführer* Muhsfeldt's petty bourgeois home in Mannheim, for that was where it was due to be sent at the end of the week. There it would wait until the stalwart *Oberscharführer* returned to lie down and rest after a hard fought war.

I was in Muhsfeldt's room that week and noticed probably half a dozen silk pyjamas laid out ready to be packed. No doubt they were also destined for his home as accessories to the bed.

Fancy foreign goods. In Germany everything was rationed. In the crematorium, however, Muhsfeldt was at liberty to pick and choose from the manifold items left behind by his victims in the undressing room. And there was just one price for everything: a shot in the back of the head from his six-millimetre gun. This replaced ration cards at the crematorium. For each murdered victim an SS-man could get jewellery, leather coats, fur coats, silks, elegant shoes. A week didn't go by without a parcel being sent home containing kilograms of tea, coffee, chocolate, tinned food. They could get everything here.

These seemingly unlimited opportunities had inspired the *Oberscharführer* to have a special bed made and delivered to his home.

Over the days, as I observed the construction of this bed, an idea also occurred to me. And gradually this idea developed into a fully fledged plan.

We were all due to die soon. There was no doubt about it. We had all got accustomed to the thought, we knew there was no escape. One thing, however, would not put my mind at rest. Eleven *Sonderkommandos* had been exterminated so far and all their members had taken with them the terrible secret of the crematoria and the pyres. This time we could not allow this to happen! We had to think of a way by which, after we were gone, the world would learn the truth about how the 'superior race' had built a system of unspeakable cruelty and depravation.

The world had to know about this, and the message could come from here! Years might pass before it happened, but when it did, it would provide incriminating evidence. The two hundred *Sonderkommando* members at Crematorium I could sign a document. We could smuggle it out of the camp in the bed and then it would remain hidden in *Oberscharführer* Muhsfeldt's Mannheim home, but only for a limited time.

And so the document was produced. It described in detail the atrocities perpetrated at the camp in the preceding years. We named the culprits. We stated the numbers of victims as well as the methods and tools of mass murder. The *Sonderkommando* scribe, a French graphic artist, recorded it all in the exquisite calligraphic style of ancient manuscripts, using India ink on three large sheets of parchment paper. A fourth sheet bore the signatures of the two hundred *Sonderkommando* members. The sheets were then bound together with fine silk, scrolled up and inserted inside a cylinder sleeve specially made by the metalworkers. The tube was hermetically sealed with solder, to protect the document from the adverse effects of air and water, and the joiners the fitted it in between the mattress springs.

We also encased an identical document bearing the same signatures in a metal container and buried it in the courtyard of Crematorium II[42].

XXII

Every day, around seven in the evening, a lorry drove in through the crematorium gate. It always delivered some seventy to eighty women or men for extermination. They were the daily quota of those selected from among the inmates of concentration camp barracks or hospitals, prisoners who had been there for at least a few months, if not years, and therefore had no illusions as to their fate. When the lorry arrived, the whole courtyard was filled with the ghastly sound of the terrified screaming of those who were about to die. The selected prisoners were fully aware of the fact that there was no escape once you were at the foot of the crematorium chimney. I did not wish to observe these scenes. As a general rule I would withdraw to the farthest corner of the courtyard and hide in a clump of pine trees where you couldn't hear the gunshots and the sound of the screams was muffled.

One evening, however, I was unlucky. I had been working in the dissecting room since five in the afternoon: I had to explain the circumstances leading to a certain *Oberscharführer's* suicide. The body had been brought from Gliwice. Present at the autopsy were a court-martial judge, a *Hauptsturmführer* SS and an SS clerk. It was around seven and I was dictating the autopsy findings to the SS clerk when a huge lorry full of male prisoners entered the courtyard. The dissecting room had two large windows with a green, wire mosquito mess looking out onto the courtyard. The lorry stopped very close these windows. The unfortunate passengers were very quiet, from which I deduced that they had not been selected from a barracks but from a hospital. They must have all been very sick, too weak to scream or even clamber down off the vehicle's high platform. The SS guards were yelling and hurrying them on, but no one moved. Finally the non-commissioned officer who had been driving the lorry lost patience and got back in behind the steering wheel. He started the engine, and then the front end of the platform gradually began to rise. The prisoners were literally tipped out. The sick and the dying fell head or face first, one on top of the other, onto the concrete. There erupted a terrifying cry as they now writhed convulsively on the ground. It was a scene from hell!

The vulgar cursing and shouting caught the attention of the SS officer, who asked me what was going on outside. While I was explaining, he approached the window. What he saw clearly shocked him, for in a disapproving tone he said: 'Still and all, they shouldn't do that...'

The *Sonderkommando* were already pulling the clothes off the victims and flinging them onto a pile in the middle of the courtyard. The naked unfortunates were carried into the crematorium building, where *Oberscharfüher* Muhsfeldt was already waiting for them in front of the ovens. Today it was his turn. He was wearing rubber gloves and holding a gun. The people were brought before him one after the other, and one after the other they fell dead on the floor. Their bodies were immediately removed to make room for the next victims. Within a few minutes Muhsfeldt had 'toppled' all eighty prisoners – '*umgelegt*' is the term they used for it. Half an hour later a handful of dust was all that remained of them.

Later that same evening the *Oberscharfüher* came to my room and requested me to examine him. He felt he had an erratic heartbeat and was suffering from headaches. I checked his blood pressure, took his pulse and listened to his heart. There was no cause for concern. I didn't find anything out of the ordinary. Only his pulse was slightly faster than normal. I suggested that it could be on account of the work he had done just half an hour earlier in the cremating room. I said this just to put his mind at rest, but my words actually had the exact opposite effect.

In his indignation he got up and standing before me, declared:

'Your diagnosis is wrong. It is of no concern to me if I shoot eighty or a thousand people. It doesn't upset me in the slightest. Do you know why I am so nervous? It's because I drink too much!'

With that he left my room, clearly disappointed.

XXIII

I usually read in bed before going to sleep. That particular evening I did the same, but I couldn't read for long because the light suddenly went out. Then I heard the air raid siren. On such occasions SS-men armed to the teeth led us down to the *Sonderkommando's* air raid shelter: the gas chamber. And it was no different on this occasion. We got dressed and descended the stairs.

I entered the dark gas chamber with a heavy heart. There were two hundred of us in there. The entire *Kommando*! It was a horrible feeling when you were fully conscious of the fact that hundreds of thousands of people had been murdered in this very same place. Even more so for when we realised that it was going to be our turn soon and the SS could easily use a similar situation to slam shut the door, and murder us all with just four tins of Zyklon.

Something like this had happened before. Part of *Sonderkommando* nine were sent to Block 13 in section D [BIId]. This was a specially isolated barracks. The *Sonderkommando* members were told that on the order of a higher authority they were to be quartered not in the crematorium but in the camp itself. From there they would go to work in two shifts at the crematorium. That same evening they were taken to get washed and get a change of clothes at one of the bathhouses in section D [BIId]. After their wash they were driven still naked into a neighbouring chamber, ostensibly to put on disinfected clothes. It was indeed a disinfecting chamber, hermetically sealed from the outside and normally used to fumigate prisoners' louse-infested clothes. This time, however, it was used to gas four hundred *Sonderkommando* members. Their bodies were then loaded onto lorries and driven to the blazing ditches.

So we had a very good reason to be extremely tense all the time until the all clear was sounded. The air raid lasted three hours. We emerged from the darkness. The arc lights were once again illuminating the many kilometres of barbed-wire fences. We went to bed. I tried to sleep, but it wasn't easy.

Doing my rounds the next day I visited Crematorium II, where the *Sonderkommando's Oberkapo* informed me confidentially that during the previous night's air raid some partisans approached the camp's perimeter and cut an inconspicuous opening in the barbed-wire fence to slip through three sub-machine guns, ammunition and twenty grenades. The people of the *Sonderkommando* found it early in the morning and had hidden the weapons in a safe place.

There appeared a chink of light in our dark prospects. We knew that those who had smuggled for us these weapons could not be far off. Numerous observations suggested that the partisans had set up their camp some 25-30 kilometres from where we were. We hoped that during the next air raid they would deliver firearms once more. For now there were air raids every day, frequently several times a day. However, we could only expect our anonymous friends to come in the night during long blackouts. It would take three or four night raids for the partisans to supply us with enough arms to organise a breakout.

The underground movement had begun in Crematorium III and thence spread its network to the remaining crematoria. Everything was organised with great care and discretion. Death came very easily from the barrel of a sub-machine gun and we wanted to live. We wanted to break out and be free! If only one or two of us succeeded, we would still have won, for then the world would discover the terrible secret of the death factory. We did not want to be crushed like worms beneath the boots of our executioners. We wanted to go down in the history of the German death camps as those who perished fighting and even inflicting death to the oppressors.

XXIV

One day I was talking to *Oberschafführer* Steinberg. He frequently visited me in the dissecting room. In the days of the Weimar Republic he used be a traffic policeman in Berlin, with the coming of the Third Reich he joined the SS. In my opinion, this was a particularly dangerous man, for apart from his decidedly criminal nature, he was also quite intelligent. He told me that four of them were going on leave to an SS leisure home in Silesia – the other three being *Oberschafführer* Seitz, *Rottenführer* Hollander and *Rottenführer* Eidenmüller[43]. I knew all four well, they were the crematoria's cruellest killers, and Steinberg was now telling me that they had received five days leave. I had been in the *Sonderkommando* three months now, so I knew that when an SS-man was telling me that something was black, even though it might seem to me to be black, I was not allowed to believe it. If *Oberschafführer* Steinberg talked of being granted leave, then there was no doubt that he had been in fact given a particularly bloody task to fulfil. I was convinced of this because I knew that the SS crematorium staff had been forbidden to leave their quarters, no doubt so that they didn't disclose anything about the crime over a few glasses with drinking companions. They could only leave and return to their posts in a company commanded by an officer. Though there were certain differences, they were also a *Sonderkommando* of sorts. I had heard that after two years' service they were sent to a special SS camp. This was a camp where the Third Reich exterminated those members of the SS who broke discipline, or those who simply knew too much.

Five days later *Oberschaführer* Steinberg and his three colleagues returned from leave. I asked no questions and he did not say anything either. The day they returned I went to the *Sonderkommando* kitchen, where a French cook by the name of Michel always had something good for his guests to eat. Michel was an interesting character in the *Sonderkommando*. In civilian life he used to also be a chef, working on a luxury French liner that sailed to Brazil. I found Michel, the provider of tasty morsels, in the kitchen as expected. However, this time he wasn't as hospitable as usual. It immediately became clear that something was troubling him. The pipe that he would continually puff at was now out, although he still gripped it firmly in his teeth, and the expression on his face was dour. If he had not noticed the pipe goes out, then he had to be deeply upset about something. My supposition was correct. I had barely shut the door, when he came up to me and without saying a word pulled me towards a corner of the room where there was a metal washtub on a stool. With two fingers, he pulled out of the water first one, then second and then a third green SS shirt. All three shirts were deeply stained with blood, one could only get a shirt so bloody in a slaughterhouse. Thus *Oberschaführer* Steinberg and his three colleagues must have spent their five days' leave in an abattoir, in an abattoir where they slaughtered humans. Michel told me that they had given him the shirts to wash immediately after their return.

I therefore do not exaggerate in the conviction not believe an SS-man who told you that something was black even if it might also seem be black to you.

XXV

The hour had come for the 4,500 inhabitants of the Gypsy camp. The process of annihilation was carried out in exactly same way as it had been in the case of the Czech camp. All prisoners had been confined to barracks and numerous SS formations, including dog handlers, brought in. Next the Gypsies were flushed out of their blocks and made to line up. They were told that they were being moved to another camp, and even though the Gypsies had now been inmates for two years, they believed this because each one of them receives a three-day ration of bread, ostensibly for a three-day journey. A very simple yet effective trick. The duped Gypsies didn't even suspect that they were being led to the crematorium, for would those sent to die be given bread?

Of course, the SS command did not issue an order to give prisoners bread out of any humanitarian considerations. In this case it was simply a ploy to take a large mass of people to the gas chamber under the smallest possible escort, in the greatest order and in the least time wasted.

And this was indeed what happened. The chimneys of crematoria I and II illuminated the entire camp throughout the night with their fire. The Gypsy camp that had been teeming with life was now empty and silent. Now only the wind blew in among the deserted barracks, slamming the shutters and doors, and singing on the barbed wire. Once again Europe's pyromaniacs had organized a gigantic display of fireworks. Once again the setting was the Auschwitz concentration camp. This time, however, the victims thrown to the flames were not Jews, but Christians: Catholics Gypsies from Germany and Austria. The flames died down towards dawn. Instead their appeared silvery, glimmering piles in the crematorium courtyards – the victims' ashes.

However, the corpses of twenty-four twins did not end up in the ovens. Even before they perished in the gas chamber, Dr Mengele had written on their chests with a special ink two letters: ZS (*zur Sektion*) – which meant that they were to be dissected!

There was now a collection of twin corpses representing all ages from new-born babes to sixteen-year-olds. The dark-skinned bodies of these dark-haired children were lying on the concrete floor. I had a difficult job in matching the pairs, brother next to brother, sister next to sister. And I had to be very careful not to muddle them up, since Dr Mengele would punish a mistake that wasted such valuable research material with death. I could be certain of that on account of what had happened the day before when we were sitting together at my desk, going over some files on twins that had already been dissected. There was a very slight grease mark on one of them which Dr Mengele happened to notice. I had frequently referred to these files during autopsies and so it was quite natural that such marks would occur. Mengele looked at me reproachfully and with great gravity said: 'How can you treat in such a way files that I have collected with such love?'

His lips had actually uttered the word 'love'. The shock left me dumbstruck.

XXVI

One day I was dissecting the body of an elderly man and I found some interesting stones in his gallbladder. Knowing that Dr Mengele was an avid collector of such items, I rinsed, dried and then placed them in a hermetically sealed jar. I also attached a label with the man's personal details, including his medical record. I gave the jar to Doctor Mengele the following day during his morning visit. He was very pleased and examined the gallstones from all angles. And then, quite out of the blue, he turned to me and asked: 'Do you know the ballad of Prince Wallenstein?' His question was inappropriate. Nonetheless, I responded by saying that although knew of Wallenstein, I had never heard of a ballad about him. Whereupon Mengele smiled and recited as follows:

Im Besitze der Familie Wallenstein
Ist mehr Gallenstein, wie Edelstein...
Which can be roughly translated:
In the Wallenstein family's possession
There were more gallstones than precious stones...

He recited this facetious verse with such good humour that I decided it was a opportune moment to make an exceptionally bold advance.

I asked him if could see my wife and daughter! I immediately realised the risk I was taking, but it was too late, I had said it. He looked at me astounded.

'You have a wife, and a child?' he asked.

'Yes, *Herr Haupsturmführer*, I have a wife and a fifteen-year-old daughter,' I replied, somewhat flustered.

'And you think they are still here?'

'I think so because three months ago, when we arrived here, you told them to join the column on the right.'

'But it's possible that since then they have been sent to another camp,' he conjectured.

I looked out of the window, towards the crematorium chimneys... Doctor Mengele sat at the desk leaning on one elbow. I was standing beside him and could see that he was thinking.

'I'll give you a *Passierschein*, you may look for them, *but...*' he raised a forefinger to his lips and looked at me. The look and gesture were menacing.

'I understand, thank you very much, *Herr Haupsturmführer*.'

Doctor Mengele left and I retired to my room clutching the *Passierschein*. Then I read it: 'Prisoner A 8450 is authorised move around freely in KL Auschwitz territory without an escort. The above order is to remain valid until cancelled.' Signed: Dr Mengele, *Haupsturmführer* SS.

I felt extremely agitated. Probably in the entire history of the camp up until that moment no prisoner had ever been granted permission to search for his family and enter a women's sector without an escort.

I didn't even know where to begin. Women prisoners were kept in camp sections C [BIIc], BIII and FKL[44]. It was, however, my understanding that most of the women from Hungary had been sent to section C [BIIc]. There were probably some fifty thousand of them there now. So that was where I'd start!

The next day I got up feeling tired. I hadn't slept all night. Those terrible doubts kept me awake. Three months was a long time, especially in a concentration camp where even an hour could last ages. A lot had happened since we arrived at Auschwitz, and I knew better than anyone else how much could happen there during every hour of every day.

I entered the SS-men's room and reported my departure. I said farewell to my companions. They all wished me luck.

On a hot, sunny August morning I set off on my three-kilometre trek. As the crow flies, section C [BIIc] was actually much closer, but to get there I had to go around a security cordon and bypass various other sectors on the way. With a sense of trepidation and curiosity I proceeded down the path in-between the sections, marked out by the high voltage barbed-wire fences. The guards in the watchtowers were forbidden to shoot at anyone on this path without first issuing a warning, and only SS-men on motorcycles patrolled these routes.

In fact I encountered numerous patrols on the way, but somehow none of them was interested in stopping me. And so I reached section C [BIIc]. I was confronted by a huge iron gate with a dense mesh of barbed wire held in place by porcelain insulators. As at the entrance to every other section, there was a *Blockführerstube* in front of the gate. A few SS-men were sitting outside on a bench, basking in the sunlight. They eyed me up and down. My presence there must have been quite an unusual sight for them, but they said nothing. They were not going to impinge on the authority of their colleague sitting at the guardhouse window. I approached him and read out my tattooed camp number. He stared at me inquiringly, so I took the pass bearing Doctor Mengele's signature out of my pocket and showed it to him. The SS-guard read it and then issued the command to his colleagues. The camp-section gates opened. Meanwhile the SS-guard enquired how long I intended to stay in the section, for I had to return at a predetermined time. I glanced at my watch: it was ten o'clock. So I told the SS-guard I would be back by twelve noon, which was what he entered in the register. That was actually quite a long time, but in such situations a box of ten Josma cigarettes served as well as a pass in any part of the camp. I gave him the cigarettes and enter the sector.

A lot was going on in the main street in between the green barracks of section C [BIIc]. A group of women were carrying a huge metal barrel full of hot soup, because the inmates' dinner was always brought out from the kitchen already at ten. Another women's *Kommando* was carrying cobblestones. On either side of the road there were large numbers of women with shaven heads, wrapped in rags, crouching or lying on the ground in the sunlight. It was a pitiful sight. Most of them were grotesquely dressed: very long, low-cut, sleeveless evening dresses. And in such clothes they were trying to eradicate lice. Some were picking these parasites off their companions. Their bodies were dirty and covered with festering abscesses.

This was a quarantine camp. Here the women didn't work. Instead a proportion of them was selected for transports out of Auschwitz to work in other camps. I could see that this group had already undergone many selections. Those who remained were clearly ill-suited for hard labour. Lucky were the ones that got onto the transports! At least they still had a slight chance of surviving. On the other hand, the fate of those unfortunates still at Auschwitz was sealed, as in the case of the Gypsy and Czech camps.

I headed for the first barracks. I was greeted with a racket of voices screeching and shouting. The rag-clad spectres lying on the floor suddenly stirred, the terrifying figures rose up and rushed towards me. There must have been about thirty of them: they realised who I was and all at once started eagerly asking me for information about their husbands and children.

They were able to recognise me because I still looked civilised and human, but they had changed beyond all recognition. More and more women surrounded me, and each one desperately wanted to know about their family. They had been there for three months now, living in terrible conditions and in constant fear. There had been a selection every week. Three months in a concentration camp made them mourn the past and dread the future. These unfortunate women were also asking me about the rumours concerning the crematoria. They wanted to know the meaning of the black smoke during the daytime and the huge flames seen there at night. They wanted me to confirm whether they were really burning people. I tried to put their minds at rest as best I could by denying everything. I told them that all these rumours were untrue. Besides the war was almost over and we would all soon be able to return home. I didn't believe a word of what I was saying, but I wanted to calm them down. I left them not having found out anything about my own family: my wife and daughter.

I entered the next barracks and this time asked the block overseer, who happened to be a Slovak girl, to call out my wife's surname. In one such barracks there were from 800 to 1,000 women, crammed together in long tiered rows of berths on either side of an aisle. It was very difficult to make oneself heard in such a block. The overseer's voice was drowned out by the din. She returned after a while, her efforts had turned out to be futile. Nonetheless, I thanked her and moved on to the next barracks. The situation there was the same as in the previous block, and once again the same scene unfolded. Here too my search proved fruitless. In the subsequent barracks I stood in the centre of the aisle and asked someone to summon the overseer. When she came I told her that I was searching for my wife and daughter, whereupon the overseer dispatched two bright little girls to look for them. They proceeded down both sides of the aisle, shouting out our family name at each berth, and then... they started heading back, bringing with them my wife and daughter!

They approached me holding hands, their eyes wide open with fright – it was usually a bad omen when you were summoned in a concentration camp. Then they recognised me. They now stood rooted to the ground. I ran towards them and started hugging and kissing both of them at once. They said nothing, but they were silently weeping – shedding very bitter tears. I calmed them down. By then a crowd of inquisitive prisoners had gathered around us, so I turned to the block overseer and asked if she could let us into her room. At last we were alone.

They now started telling me about their traumatic experiences of the preceding three months in the camp: of the terrifying selections, of the constant fear when living in the shadow of the crematorium chimneys. They were malnourished, and exposed to the elements in their tattered clothes. The barrack roof leaked and when it was raining, it was impossible for them to dry their clothes. The food was virtually inedible. What was worse, they couldn't even sleep properly at nights. A single berth was intended for seven people, yet at present there were twelve in each. My daughter told me that in recent weeks she had had to sleep in a couched position on the concrete floor because there was not enough room for her on the bunk.

My wife asked me where I was working. I told her that I was Doctor Mengele's assistant at the crematorium and a member of the *Sonderkommando*. Having already been three months in the camp, they knew that the *Sonderkommando* was a squad of prisoners condemned to die. So the news appalled them. I did my best to reassure them. Then I had to leave, but I promised to return again the next day.

The crematorium was astir with the news that I had found my wife and daughter. I had my rucksack packed with warm underwear, stockings and other items of clothing from the clothes department; and from another department: toothbrushes, soap, nail clippers, some penknives and fine combs. On top of that, I took medicines, vitamins, a salve for wounds, some dressings, everything that was necessary or could be necessary. Furthermore, I took enough sugar lumps, butter, apricot jam and bread to be shared with other prisoners. Laden with all these goods, the next day I headed off once more to section C [BIIc]. From then on I was there every day with a full sack.

But alas all good things come to an end. I had been at section C [BIIc] every day for two weeks. Then came the moment that I was dreading. After the liquidation of the Czech and Gypsy camps I came to the conclusion that it was only a matter of days when the same fate would befall section C [BIIc]. After all, sooner or later everyone who was unfortunate enough to end up in KL Auschwitz became a victim of liquidation.

One afternoon I was sitting at the laboratory bench together with Dr Thilo and Dr Mengele. The two SS doctors were talking and the topic of their conversation were the concentration camp's administrative problems. Suddenly Dr Mengele got up and in a determined voice declared to Dr Thilo:

'I can no longer afford to feed those feeble, unproductive inhabitants of camp C. They shall be liquidated within two weeks!'

Such conversations frequently took place in my presence. They discussed the most confidential matters concerning the camp as if I weren't there. After all, I was in fact condemned to die, I no longer counted, I had practically ceased to exist.

Doctor Mengele's terrifying decision was a very heavy blow to me. Not only the lives of my closet family but also of thousands of my compatriots was now at stake. I had to act at once!

No sooner had doctors Mengele and Thilo left the crematorium building then I, too, was beyond the gate. My path led to section D [BIId]. This was where the *Arbeitseinsatz* was situated, the office that allocated prisoner labour. It was this department that carried out the selections of prisoners and sent them to work in labour camps and factories located throughout the Third Reich that supported the German war effort.

The man in charge of this department was an SS *Oberscharführer*. He was alone in his office. I introduced myself and showed him my permanent *Passierschein*, which had been issued by Dr Mengele. I told him that my wife and daughter were currently in section C [BIIc]. I had managed to trace them with Doctor Mengele's help and was now helping them with what means I had at my disposal. However, I urgently felt that that they should leave Auschwitz as soon as possible, for, being employed at the crematorium, I was perfectly aware of what awaited those who remained in the camp for too long. The manager of this department fully agreed with my reasoning and promised to help. That week there were two transports due to be selected from section C [BIIc]. Each was to take three thousand people to munitions plants in western Germany. Such plants were relatively good workplaces because extermination was not part of their policy. People there were provided with adequate living conditions, food and generally treated in such a way so as to maintain their value as a manual workforce; the overriding objective was to maximise output. I pulled out of my pocket a box of a hundred cigarettes and placed it on the table. The SS-man took it and promised to admit my wife and daughter to one of the transports, provided, of course, that they volunteered during the selection. I had got what I wanted!

I hurried towards section C [BIIc] with a difficult task to fulfil. I had to somehow convince my dearest ones that they had to leave the camp without actually telling them the real reason why. I couldn't tell the truth, for that would have started a panic with probably fatal consequences for all of them.

I took my wife and daughter to the block overseer's room. I told them that although it was very hard for me to part company with them, it was imperative that they left Auschwitz. We had to stop seeing each other, I had to give up looking after them, the situation demanded it. I told them that during that week the SS would select prisoners from their section for two huge transports. They had to volunteer to go with one of them, preferably the first.

I explained to my wife that there was a very good reason which compelled me to advise them in such a way. I also asked her to tell all our friends to volunteer for the transports, but to say nothing more then that.

When making up transports, the SS selecting commission first chose from those prisoners who volunteered and only then completed the required quota with prisoners selected by force. Usually very few prisoners volunteered because most feared that they would be letting themselves in for something even worse than their current wretched conditions. Besides, who would volunteer to work on meagre rations that were already insufficient in the quarantine camp where they didn't have to work. Those poor wretches! They did not understand the morality of Third Reich concentration camps, they did not realise that those who did not work were not allowed to live!

My wife and daughter understood that I must have had very valid reasons to advise them as I did. They promised me that they would volunteer at the next selection.

I left them, vowing that in two days I would return to bring warm clothes and victuals for the journey.

The two days went by and with a heavy heart I set out for section C [BIIc] to say my final farewell. I took with me plenty of clothes and food. But this time I did not go alone. I would not have dared to take so many things past the gate to section C [BIIc], for there could always be some SS officers in the vicinity. That was why I had asked an SS-man from the crematorium, a patient whom I had cured of pneumonia, to accompany me and help throw the parcels over the fence.

I could not enter the barracks, so I summoned my wife and daughter to come out and approach the barbed-wire perimeter. Then my SS escort and I threw the parcels over the fence. Fortunately, there was no one nearby to notice what we were doing.

We were kept apart by barbed wire. We couldn't even embrace. We just talked for a few minutes. My wife told me that they had no problems with volunteering. They didn't even need to report their names to the *Oberscharführer* in charge of the selection. Instead they were immediately put onto the transport list. My joy was all the greater when she added that many other women had followed her advice and also opted to join the transport.

XXVII

Three days later I went one more time to section C [BIIc] to assure myself that my wife and daughter had indeed left the camp.

Everything happened as I desired. Two transports – comprising three thousand women each – departed from Auschwitz concentration camp, taking those most dear to me. Although I couldn't possibly know what the future held in store for them, for me it was still a great relief. At Auschwitz there was only certain death, whereas from their new destination, with a bit of luck, they would eventually be set free! There were now many signs that the war was coming to an end. The grave for the Third Reich was already being dug. Those who had managed to get out of Auschwitz could once again afford to hope. I, on the other hand, was fully aware of the hopelessness of my own situation.

I felt deep satisfaction in that fact that I had managed to save my dearest ones from the Auschwitz pyres. Nonetheless, I sensed the inevitability and imminence of my own death here. Neither fear nor despair led me to this conclusion; instead it was knowledge of the bloody tragedies that had befallen the previous eleven *Sonderkommandos* and my own, cold, dispassionately logical reasoning. Walking away from section C [BIIc], I cast my eyes back once more to the gloomy barracks. It was with painful sadness that I said goodbye to the place where wretched, haggard figures with shaven heads drifted about in their rags, deprived of all human dignity. Grotesque figures that were once our beautiful wives and daughters.

A chill ran down my spine, and soon my whole body was shivering. I wrapped myself up in my coat and only then realised that it was already autumn. September, a strong northern wind was blowing towards the already snow-capped Beskidy Mountains, rattling the barbed wire and fanning the flames coming out of the crematorium chimneys. Here and there a few crows flew by, the only birds to be seen at Auschwitz. The wind carried in my direction wisps smoke from the stacks of crematoria that had been built to last for centuries. The familiar stench of burning flesh and hair.

The days and nights went by in idleness and restless anticipation. I was silent, I had no further desires. I felt how my loneliness had been choking me ever since my dearest ones had left. I was tormented by my own helplessness.

Silence and interminable monotony had descended on Auschwitz concentration camp. This was a bad sign! My intuition had never failed me before. This great silence heralded the imminence of even greater bloodshed. The twelfth *Sonderkommando* had used up the three and a half months of its four-month life span. The sands of time were running out fast. We had only two weeks left...

Doctor Mengele was true to his word. Sector C [BIIc] was liquidated. Every evening fifty lorries transported forty thousand victims to the crematoria. It was an appalling sight: long columns of trucks with their headlights on, driving into the crematorium courtyard and carrying their human cargo which was either screaming dementedly or petrified with terror.

The wretched victims were already naked when they unloaded them right in front of the entrance leading down to the gas chamber. All the women knew perfectly well that they were about to be gassed, but over the four preceding months they had had prison discipline drummed into them and experienced nervous breakdowns, suffering that weaken their bodies and souls and deprived them of any will to resist. They simply allowed themselves to be herded into the gas chambers, where a cruel death awaited them. Nevertheless, it ended for each of them what was by then a pointless, unbearable life.

And how long the road had been before it came to this! And how inhuman, incomprehensible was the suffering they were subjected to at each stage of the journey! Their peaceful, family homes were ransacked and razed to the ground. Together with their husbands, children and elderly parents they were rounded up in the ghetto, in an old brickyard on the outskirts of town, where for weeks they were all forced to lie in the puddles left by the spring rains. And every day groups of them were taken to be interrogated in specially set up torture chambers, where they had their fingers crushed and were beaten with rubber truncheons until they revealed where and with whom they had hidden their valuables. Many died as a consequence of these torture sessions. The rest where then packed into boxcars, eighty or ninety in each. And in such conditions they travelled for four to five days, together with the corpses of those who had died on the way, until the train finally pulled up alongside the ramp at Auschwitz.

We already know what happened next. Traumatised by the fact that they had been separated from their closest family, the women ended up in the barracks of section C [BIIc]. Yet before they entered this filthy hotbed of lice and disease, they had first to undergo a procedure that stripped them of the remaining vestiges of human dignity – the bathhouse ritual. Coarse hands ripped their clothes off and cropped their hair. After the shower they were handed new clothes which the poorest beggar would have thrown away with disgust. And together with these rags, their first actual gift from the Third Reich: lice.

Thus our wives, mothers, sisters and daughters began their languishing existence behind concentration-camp barbed wire. The food was worse than pigs' swill. It prevented them from starving to death and yet it was still barely adequate to support life. It was devoid of protein. The lack of this vital nutrient made their legs feel as heavy as lead. The deficiency of fat caused swelling and the disruption of a normal, regular menstruation cycle resulted in vexation, headaches and frequent nosebleeds. The lack of vitamin B caused constant drowsiness and memory lose; to such an extent they would in some cases even forget the names of streets and numbers of houses were they had lived. Only in their eyes was there still a glimmer of life, or rather just hunger.

During roll call they were made to stand in rank and file for hours on end as their numbers were counted over and over again, interminably. And when they passed out and fell to the ground, a bucket of freezing water would be used to wake them up; and on reawakening, they would first look towards the clouds of black smoke and flames emitted from the crematorium chimneys. Smoke and fire were the two symbols, the constant reminder that extermination was looming over them...

For four months the inmates of section C [BIIc] had existed in the shadow of the crematorium and then it took ten days for all of them to cross its threshold.

Camp c, the site of so many tragedies, was once again silent...

XXVIII

Days, weeks, months went by. And every day the *Sonder-kommando* awaited the coming of the end. The most dreaded moment, our execution, was ever nearer. After it everything would turn into darkness and ashes... We expected the arrival of our SS executioners at any time.

On the morning of 6th October 1944[45] a shot rang out from one of the watchtowers in the neutral zone between the small and large security cordons. The mortally wounded prisoner fell to the ground. He was a Russian officer who had been sent to Auschwitz concentration camp for attempting to escape from a prisoner-of-war camp. Here, too, he had tried to escape and that was why he ended up on the receiving end of an SS guard's gun.

SS-men from the *Politische Abteilung*, headed by Doctor Mengele, arrived on site to examine an incident that was in fact an everyday occurrence. Normally the body would have been taken to the mortuary and then to the crematorium without any formalities; except this time it was the body of a Russian officer whose full name had been entered in the register. Therefore an autopsy report was necessary to corroborate evidence explaining the prisoners violent death... Having completed the *in situ* inspection, Dr Mengele had the body taken to the crematorium and issued instructions for an autopsy to be carried out. He stipulated that the report had to be ready by 2.30 and that it was to be handed to him personally, so that he could go over it.

It was around nine when Dr Mengele left the room. I asked for the corpse to be laid on the dissecting table and proceeded with the autopsy. I could have finished it within thirty to forty minutes, but it was October 6th: the last or penultimate day of this *Sonderkommando's* existence. We knew nothing for certain, but our intuition told us that death was now very close at hand. I could not work. I left the dissecting room and went to by quarters. Chain smoking and having taken an extra large dose of luminal, I still didn't know how to occupy myself. So I went to the furnace room.

The dayshift was working sluggishly although several hundred corpses were stacked up in front of the ovens. Some of them were gathered in small groups, quietly conferring about something. I went upstairs to their sleeping quarters. The nightshift would normally have had breakfast and gone to bed. This time, however, it was different. It was incredible: 10 a.m. and no one was yet asleep. Another most peculiar thing was that, although it was a mild, sunny October day, they were dressed in sports clothes, including warm jumpers and knee boots.

Everyone was either milling around or sorting the contents of their suitcases. Yet despite this apparent bustle, I sensed immense tension. Something was going to happen. I entered the *Oberkapo's* small separate room. Seated at the table were the nightshift's *Kapo*, the maintenance engineer, the chief stoker and the *Gaskommando Kapo*. I had barely sat down when they poured me half a glass of excellent Polish cumin-flavoured vodka from an already half-empty bottle. I knocked it back in one go. It might not have provided salvation in our *Sonderkommando's* final hours, but it certainly helped in overcoming the fear of death...

My companions explained our situation in detail. All the information they had gathered suggested that the *Sonderkommando* was to be liquidated the next day, or alternatively in three days' time. However, everything had been prepared for the 860[46] *Sonderkommando* members to break out of the crematoria that very night. Our escape route was to lead us to a bend in the river

Vistula some two kilometres from the camp where, after the hot summer, the water was shallow enough to wade across. And beyond the river there was an eight-kilometre stretch of forest where it would be easy to find safe hideouts for weeks, even months, and establish contact with the partisans. The weapons supplied to us by some Polish Jewish women[47] employed at the Union Munitions Factory in Oświęcim would give us a fighting chance to pull it off. Our arsenal included a hundred highly explosive ecrasite charges, which the Germans used, among other things, to blow up railway tracks. Besides that, we had five sub-machineguns[48] and twenty grenades. And that was our entire stockpile. The operation was to begin with a surprise knife-attack on the SS night watch. Next, the plan was to descend on the SS warders' dormitories and, having captured their firearms, take the remaining guards as hostages for as long as would be necessary... An electric torch was to be used to pass the escape signal on from Crematorium I to II, and then from II to III and from III to IV. To me, the whole plan seemed quite feasible. All the more so because no crematorium, apart from I, was burning bodies that day. Thus when work finished at our crematorium at six, none of the *Sonderkommandos* would be working on the nightshift. On such nights the SS posted fewer guards: only three in each crematorium. We parted company, resolving to continue working as usual and generally avoid arousing any suspicions until the signal was given.

On my way back to my room I passed the ovens again. The prisoners were working lethargically. I related the situation to my fellow physicians. I said nothing, however, to our assistant. He had been a concentration camp inmate for many years now and I didn't trust him. Either way he would have to accept the situation when it occurred.

Lunchtime approached, so my companions and I quietly consumed our meal and then went out together into the crematorium courtyard to warm ourselves in the balmy autumn sunlight. There was a conspicuous absence of SS-men. They were probably in their rooms, as had been the case many times before. The gate was closed and the guards were posted on the other side, as always. So there was really nothing untoward to worry about. I calmly smoked my cigarette. The thought that that night I could be beyond the barbed-wire fences, free, had dispelled the horrible feeling that had been weighing down on me for the preceding four months. If we failed, there was nothing to lose anyway!

I glanced at my watch. It was half past one. The autopsy had to be finished by half past two, when Dr Mengele was due to arrive. My colleagues silently followed me to the dissecting room. We set to work immediately. On that particular day one of my colleagues performed the autopsy while I typed the report.

We worked in total silence for about twenty minutes, when suddenly the whole room was shaken by a huge explosion. And then, there was a rapid exchange of sub-machinegun fire.

Peering through the green mess of one of the large dissecting-room windows, I saw the red roof of Crematorium III collapsing in on itself[49]. Wooden beams and bricks were thrown up into the air and soon there was a huge column of black smoke and flames. Barely a minute passed when sub-machinegun fire erupted just outside our door.

I had no idea of what could have happened. It was all supposed to have started at night. Perhaps we'd been betrayed and the SS had begun a pre-emptive attack? Or could it be that the partisans were storming the crematoria?[50]

The sirens at Auschwitz I and Auschwitz II had begun to wail. The sound of explosions and gunfire became more and more intense. We could now discern the sound of heavy-machinegun fire.

My mind was made up quickly: regardless of whether it was betrayal or a partisan attack, we had to stay put! It was the most sensible thing to do. We had to stay and wait for the situation to unfold. I could now see through the window eight or ten trucks approaching. They pulled up alongside our crematorium and I could see half a battalion of SS-men jump out and start taking up positions in front of the barbed-wire fence.

122

Now the situation was clear: the *Sonderkommando* prisoners had taken over Crematorium I and were now firing and throwing grenades from windows at the SS soldiers, who were no yet in proper formation. The prisoners' resistance was effective because I could see SS-men lying on the ground – dead or wounded. The attackers therefore tried a more efficient means. They had brought some forty or fifty trained guard dogs and now tried set them on the prisoners inside the crematorium. And yet this time, to my astonishment, I observed how these ever obedient, ferocious beasts cowered behind their SS masters, whimpering. My explanation is that these dogs had been trained to attack prisoners in striped uniforms. There were none such inside the crematorium building. Moreover, there were many things which must have been too much for the dogs' acute sense of smell: the whole area was steeped in the stench of burnt flesh, blood and bones.

The attempt to flush out the prisoners with dogs also proving a failure, the SS brought in two anti-aircraft guns from nearby positions and aimed them at the crematorium building. The *Sonderkommando* could not possibly hold out against such overwhelming firepower. A loud hurrah shook the building and the men of the *Sonderkommando* rushed out through the back entrance. Still shooting at the cordon of SS-men, the prisoners got out through the previously cut hole in the electrified barbed-wire fence and then started running towards the Vistula. An even more ferocious exchange of fire ensued between the SS and the escapees. Apart from the cracking of rifle fire, as well as the detonations of grenades and ecrasite charges, I now distinctly heard the sound of the heavy machineguns on the watchtowers joining in.

After less than ten minutes things quietened down.

A preliminary bombardment from the anti-aircraft guns no longer necessary, the SS soldiers stationed around the crematorium began their assault on the building. With bayonets fixed, they rushed in from all sides and quickly occupied the rooms on all the floors.

Ten SS-men burst into the dissecting room. Their guns pointed at us, we were surrounded and with hands raised, amid blows from rifle butts, pushed out into the courtyard. There all four of us were ordered to lie flat on the ground face down. 'And whosoever should just move or raise his head, gets a bullet in it!' added the SS-man.

A few minutes later I heard the sound of many feet heading in our direction – I assumed it to be a large group of captured *Sonderkommando* men. They were all ordered to lie down on the ground around us. How many of them could there have been? I was unable find to out because we were all lying in a single row. Three or four minutes later a new group was brought into the courtyard and again ordered to lie down with the rest of us.

We were all lying motionless in the courtyard, while the swearing and cursing SS-men hit us with rifle butts and kicked us in the head, back and hips with their hobnailed boots. Blood trickled down my face from the back of my head and I recognised its salty taste on my lips. But I only really felt the first blows. My head felt dizzy, spinning. My mind became vacant. I was gradually losing my senses. I was slipping into non-existence.

We lay like this for twenty to thirty minutes, waiting for the SS-men standing over us to finally open fire from their sub-machineguns. I was convinced I'd get a bullet in the back of my head. It would have been the fastest and easiest way to die. I knew it all too well! I could picture it in my mind, my splattered brain and the scattered fragments of skull; the consequences of being shot at such a close range.

Then the roar of a car engine. I could only be Dr Mengele's car! It was, after all, the moment he and the men of the *Politische Abteilung* had been waiting for. I couldn't raise my head to see but I recognised the voice. He was talking to the commander standing directly in front of us. Suddenly a sonorous voice rang out. One of the SS-men was shouting:

'Physicians, get up!'

We obeyed. All four of us stood to attention and waited for what was to happen next. Doctor Mengele summoned me. There was blood all over my face and shirt, my clothes were covered in mud. And in such a state I had to stand before him.

'What have you done?' inquired Dr Mengele.

'Nothing, sir' I replied, 'We were only carrying out your orders, *Herr Hauptsturmführer*. We were actually in the middle of doing the autopsy of the Russian officer when it all broke out. And so we had to interrupt our work, the autopsy report is still in the typewriter. Everyone can confirm this! We stayed at our workplace all the time, and that is where they found us.'

The SS commander confirmed that this was true. So Dr Mengele turned to me and said:

'Please go and wash yourself, and continue with your work!' He gave the sign for the other three physicians to follow.

I turned round and headed for the crematorium door, my three colleagues following on behind me. We had hardly taken a few paces when there was a sudden burst of sub-machinegun fire behind our backs. The men of the *Sonderkommando* were all shot dead.

I did not look back. I just walked on faster, all the way to my room. With trembling hands I tried to roll up a cigarette. I wasted three cigarette papers before finally succeeding. I lit my rollup, took a deep drag and staggered to my bed. Only when I lay down did I start to feel the pain of the blows and kicks I had received.

So much had happened that day! And it was still barely three in the afternoon. The fact that I had survived gave me no sense of joy or relief. My life had only been briefly prolonged. I knew the mentality of people like Dr Mengele and the SS. They had simply realised that they still needed the work I was carrying out and that I was difficult to replace. There was no other specialist in the camp who would meet Dr Mengele's rigorous requirements. Even if there were such a person, he would in all probability never wish to reveal himself for fear of getting into Dr Mengele's clutches and ending up as a member of the *Sonderkommando*.

Once my nerves had recovered a little from the trauma, I got up from my bed to have a look round. I wanted to find out what had happened in the afternoon. Had there indeed been a traitor in our midst and had the SS consciously taken pre-emptive action against the planned revolt and escape of the *Sonderkommando*? There could hardly have been a better pretext to exterminate it. My other hypothesis was that the *Sonderkommando's* lease on life was due to end that very day and that the SS-men of the *Politische Abteilung* for this reason had been instructed to liquidate it. They had summoned a roll call, ostensibly just to check that all the prisoners were present but in actual fact in order to execute them. That had been the SS method used on every *Sonderkommando* so far. But it did not happen that way with the twelfth: our *Kommando* put up armed resistance.

The bodies of my dead companions were now lying stripped naked in a long row in front of the ovens. One by one, I recognised those who had managed to break out of Crematorium I. They fell trying break through subsequent lines of fire. Their bodies had been carted in on wheelbarrows. I also saw those companions who were shot in the courtyard just after we had left. After the revolt had been quashed they were rounded up in crematoria II, III and VI and taken here to be killed, then burnt with the others, for on that day only the ovens at Crematorium I were working and the SS had at its disposal only thirty hastily recruited members of the new *Sonderkommando*.

I was standing beside an SS non-commissioned officer who was taking down the dead men's camp numbers as the newly recruited prisoners turned their bodies face up. Without my asking, he declared that twelve men were still unaccounted for. Apart from seven, all the rest were dead. We three physicians and our dissecting room assistant were four of these seven known survivors. The other people whose lives had been spared were the engineer, maintenance mechanic for the engines and ventilation units, one of the chief stokers and the *Pipel*, that is a messenger and general dog's body whom the SS employed to clean their clothes and shoes, wash the dishes and mind the telephone.

Twelve prisoners had managed to escape.

The *Pipel* was able to tell me in detail what had actually happened that day.

Betrayal was out of the question. At half past one in the afternoon trucks bearing seventy SS-men arrived at Crematorium III. They were from a special detachment. The commander of this detachment summoned all the *Sonderkommando* prisoners to come out, but no one moved. Then the SS officer decided resort to a deceptive measure – after all the SS were past masters in mendacity. He went out into the middle of the courtyard and improvised a crude and short, SS-style speech:

'People, the order here states that because you have worked hard, you will now be moved to a labour camp. There you will receive good clothes, lots of food and light work. The men whose numbers I read out are to come forward and form a line!'

Next he proceeded to read out the numbers. There were a hundred Hungarians at Crematorium III and their numbers were called out first. These were the newest prisoners at the camp and they meekly obeyed the order. There was more fear than courage in them. A group of SS-men immediately escorted the Hungarians out of the courtyard. They were locked up in Block 13 of section D [BIId].

After they had been taken away, the calling out of numbers at Crematorium III continued. It was now the turn of the Greeks. These were discernibly less willing to follow SS-man's order and stand in line as the prisoners before them had done. Then came the turn of the Poles. As their numbers began to be called out angry murmuring erupted in that group and then some of them even started shouting. The SS-man read out the next number. No one moved!

As the officer was looking round to see what the problem was, a mineral-water bottle suddenly landed at his feet. There followed and violent explosion. Seven SS-men, including the commander, fell to the ground. Some were dead, the others wounded. The bottle had been filled with ecrasite and it had been thrown by the Poles. The SS-men opened their deadly fire at the rebels, who fled back into the crematorium building. From there they started throwing more ecrasite-filled bottles out of windows onto the courtyard. Without hesitation, the SS unit shot the Greeks still standing in a line. A few of them tried to escape, but the bullets reached them at the gate.

Next, with guns constantly blazing, the SS-men proceeded to storm the entrance to Crematorium III. It was a difficult task because the Poles were putting up fierce resistance. Ecrasite-filled bottles were flying out of the windows one after the other and the powerful explosions denied access to the building.

And then there was a detonation, far stronger and more terrifying than any before, which threw to ground the SS-men who had got closest to the building. The crematorium roof burst open and amid flames and smoke hundreds of rafters were thrust high up into the air. All this had been caused by the ignition of four huge drums of petrol. The explosion devastated the building and buried the people of the Sonderkommando beneath the rubble. A few that had survived the blast continued fighting, but they soon perished in a hail of bullets from the SS sub-machineguns. The remainder – the wounded and burnt – now headed for the door with hands raised, only to be mowed down in a subsequent fusillade. They knew what awaited them, but the building was burning fiercely and so they chose the lighter death.

The one hundred Hungarians were driven back from section D [BIId] and immediately shot.

So the revolt had started in Crematorium III. Work at Crematorium I continued until the roof was blown off Crematorium III. With the sound of the explosion, the already tense atmosphere of anticipation reached its zenith. At first no one knew what had happened. The stokers left their posts to gather in a corner and begin conferring. They only had a moment to think, for one of the SS guards immediately came up to them and started berating the dayshift foreman for allowing work to be interrupted. The foreman's explanations failed to convince the guard, for the latter used all his force to strike the stoker on the head with a heavy truncheon that all the SS guards carried for the purpose of beating prisoners. From such a blow a normal person would have dropped dead with a smashed skull, but this stoker was the toughest man in the *Sonderkommando*. He just swayed a little, as blood started streaming down his face, and in the next moment pulled out a long knife from one of his knee boots and thrust it into his assailant's chest. The guard didn't even fall to ground because two other stokers immediately grabbed him. They opened the door of the first oven and shoved the SS-man into the fire.

It all happened in a flash, but the other guard was rushing towards the assembled crowd and must have noticed the SS-man's boots sticking out of the oven. He wanted to see who it was, because only *Sonderkommando* members and SS-men wore boots. However, he never did find out, for one of the prisoners stood in his way and knifed him, another two pushed him into the oven where the first SS-man was already burning.

In a few moments the prisoners had got out the sub-machine-guns, grenades and explosive charges. A ferocious gun battle ensued with the SS and *Sonderkommando* shooting at each other from opposite ends of the room.

Then in one moment a grenade exploded in among a group of SS-men – seven of them went down, either dead or no longer able to fight. There were also casualties on the *Sonderkommando* side. The fighting became even fiercer. A few more SS-men fell. The remainder – probably twenty or so – decided it would be better to withdraw from the building. They ran all the way to the gate, where they joined up with a large SS detachment that had arrived from outside.

We already know what happened next. Out of the entire crematorium *Kommando* only seven of us remained!

That evening the twelve missing prisoners were brought back. They had managed to get to the other side of the Vistula, but then there they fell into the hands of an SS unit. They were totally exhausted and had decided to stop at a house that seemed safe. The SS sprang a surprise attack and succeeded in capturing all twelve escapees alive.

I was lying in bed trying to get to sleep after the horrors of the day when I was suddenly roused by a burst of machinegun fire.

Once the shooting died down heavy steps could be heard in the corridor. The door opened and two SS-men staggered in, their faces bloody. It turned out that the moment the twelve prisoners, who were being marched back to crematorium, reached the courtyard they turned on their oppressors with bare fists in order to grab their guns. The prisoners were immediately shot.

The SS-men now wanted me to treat their injuries, and did so.

The death of my last twelve companions was a devastating blow. Having paid such a heavy price, costing so many human lives, not one prisoner had managed to escape from that godforsaken place to tell the outside world what was happening there.

However, later I found out that, despite everything, news of the *Sonderkommando's* revolt did get out. It was passed on from inmates to civilian workers employed in the camp. There were also some SS-men whose tongues wagged about what had happened.

This was an incident without precedent! A unique event in the camp's entire history. A hundred and eighty prisoners perished. On the other side, seventy SS-men were killed, including an *Obersturmführer*, seventeen *Oberscharführers* or *Scharführers* and fifty two *Sturmmans* (privates). Crematorium III was turned into rubble and Crematorium IV was put out of action because of damage to the machinery[51].

XXIX

I woke up feeling tired after a restless night. My nerves were frazzled. I was irritated even by the quietest talking of my fellow inmates or the mere sound of their footsteps.

We all went to the dissecting room in bad moods. On our way we passed the furnace room. The concrete floor was now empty. Our companions had all been burnt in the night. The ovens had now cooled down, they were barely tepid.

Thirty new men, terrified to the core by the preceding day's bloody events, lay or sat on the bunks of their predecessors. This state would only last a few days. Soon they would develop an appetite for life, and soon they too would want a tastier morsel for themselves. They'd savour the cigarettes. They'd discover that vodka was the best, most effective medicine. Alcohol for a few hours cured people of their crematorium disease. It allowed them to forget about the past and not think about the present, nor the even more terrible future. They'd now received what had been so badly lacking in the camp barracks: the wearing of proper clothes and washing to their heart's content, knowing that there was no shortage of water, soap or towels. I treated them as an old stager would treat new recruits. With time they'd get used to everything...

Because there was no work for us in the dissecting room, I instructed my colleagues to get on with anything that would help kill time. So they wiped the dust off the museum jars and glasses, sorted out the instruments and patched up the wire mesh in the windows, which had been perforated by bullets during the preceding day's gun battle. I myself sat at the table with plasters on my head, composing a list of complaints and requests that I wanted to present to Dr Mengele.

I wanted to explain to him that none of the chambers in the crematorium building were suitable for the purposes of a dissecting room, because everywhere, from all sides one could hear the deathly cries of those who were about to perish, be it by means of gassing or a shot in the back of the head, and this terrifying sound penetrated the brain. I could not set my mind to do serious research because from the moment I arrived at the crematorium I was aware of the fate of the previous eleven *Sonderkommandos* and had for four months been waiting every day, every hour for the same fate to befall the twelfth *Sonderkommando*. I also intended to ask him not give any work requiring precision, for the previous day, on 6th October 1944[52], he had ordered me to carry out and document an autopsy of a Russian officer and yet, despite this, we were attacked by an SS detachment. Artillery and dogs had been brought in. Grenades had been thrown. SS soldiers with fixed bayonets had burst into the room where we were supposed to be carrying out scientific work, beat us up, then took us out into the courtyard and ordered us to lie down on the ground. Within a few seconds I had ceased being a specialist performing an autopsy and instead became myself one of those condemned to extermination. Although it was true that Doctor Mengele had pulled me out of the group of prisoners to be imminently exterminated, I was nonetheless still in the house of death and my life had only been prolonged by a further four months. So I intended to ask him to realise that it was impossible for the current situation to persist: the previous day I had also treated two SS non-commissioned officers who hours earlier had been hitting and kicking me. They had had their guns aimed at me and were only waiting for the signal to shoot.

Such were the complaints I intended to put to my boss. My request was that we – as a four-man *Kommando* – should be moved to another place within the camp which was more suitable for our work. I had barely ordered all that I had to say in my mind, when the door opened and Dr Mengele entered the room. Complying to rules, I immediately stood to attention and, as the most senior member of the unit, declared to our superior:

'*Herr Hauptsturmführer*! I report three physicians and one laboratory assistant present at work!'

He scanned me with his eyes and fixed his gaze on my head, which was covered in plasters.

'What's happening to you?' he asked in a concerned tone. I immediately understood that he didn't want the previous day's events to be mentioned. I didn't answer his question. In fact I said very little – the mere vestiges of my catalogue of complaints, so rapidly forgotten.

'*Herr Hauptsturmführer*! This environment is unsuitable for serious scientific research. Couldn't the dissecting room be moved elsewhere?'

His face suddenly became grave.

'Are you perhaps getting sentimental?' was his chillingly curt response.

How could I have forgotten so much as to suggest to this degenerate, this research maniac a change of environment. This was where he felt best! From here one could see the burning pyres. Here the smoke rose from the crematorium chimneys. Here the walls reverberated with the screams of those being murdered and the sound of the murderers' guns. Here Dr Mengele retired after every selection and every bloody execution. Owing to his deranged 'scientific' mania, he spent all his free time here, in this terrible atmosphere, instructing me to open up the bodies of hundreds of innocent victims. Here, in a refrigerator, he kept various bacteria that were fed on fresh human meat. And here he spent hours peering into a microscope in search of the cause of a phenomenon that could never be explained: the cause of multiple births.

That day, however, he looked tired. He had returned from the Jewish ramp, where he had spent several hours in the pouring rain overseeing the selection of a large transport of Jews from the Riga ghetto. In fact there was no selection: everyone was made to join the left column. Both operational crematoria and the huge burning ditches were working to capacity. To cope with this influx, the *Sonderkommando* had to be expanded to 460 men.

My boss sat down beside one of the laboratory benches in his drenched cape. He didn't even bother to take off his peaked cap although water was dripping from it. He didn't even notice the droplets.

I offered to take his coat and cap to dry them off by the stoves.

'There's no need,' he replied, 'the water can only get as far as the skin.'

He asked me for the autopsy report on the shot Russian officer. Having taken it, he read a couple of lines and then handed it back to me.

'I'm very tired. You read it.' Astonished, I took the document, but only managed to read four or five lines when he interrupted me.

'Enough! There is no need to continue.' He said, his eyes staring blankly at the window.

What was wrong with him? Perhaps he had remembered all the perpetrated crimes? Or maybe he had received some bad news and now realised that what he was doing made no sense?

In the times spent together in the crematorium he had never given the me opportunity to talk about personal affairs. But now, when he was emotionally at such low point, I summoned up the courage to ask:

'*Herr Hauptsturmführer*, how much longer is this death an destruction going to last?'

'My friend,' he replied, 'it's going to go on, and on, and on.' His words betrayed quiet resignation. He rose from his chair to leave the laboratory.

'There'll be some interesting work for us in the next few days,' he added before departing.

A chill ran down my spine on hearing this news because 'interesting work' in all probability meant the death of a newer, larger batch of twins.

XXX

The crematoria were being made ready. The people of the Sonderkommando had replaced the brickwork inside the ovens. They had painted the heavy iron doors and oiled the hinges. The engines and ventilators were running all day because the technicians needed to make sure they worked properly. The arrival of the Łódź Ghetto had been announced.

The Łódź Ghetto[53] was set up at the end of 1939. Initially there were 500,000 inhabitants. They were forced to work in huge war factories in return for which they received so called Ghetto Marks, but they could only spend them on meagre amounts of food which also required ration cards. Hard labour together with malnutrition naturally have a wasting effect on the body. The population was decimated by frequent epidemics. Thus of the 500,000 only 70,000 remained in the autumn of 1944. And finally their time was up, too. Train loads of them started arriving at the Jewish ramp in Auschwitz. During the selections 95 percent of them went to the left, and only 5 percent to the right. Depressed by the tragedy of being separated from their families, worn out by their five years in the ghetto, they had lost all sense of reality. They calmly crossed the crematorium gate although it was no secret to them that this was the last stage of the last journey of their lives.

I went downstairs to the undressing room. Their clothes and shoes lay scattered all over the floor. No one had been interested in the clothes-hook numbers. They left their clothes on the spot where they undressed. The people sorting the clothes out opened a few parcels and showed me the contents. Cornflour pancakes, water and cooking oil, a kilogram or two of oatmeal – that was all these Jews brought with them on the journey here.

During the selection of one of the transports Dr Mengele noticed in the crowd a hunchback, around fifty years old. The cripple was not alone; standing beside him, was a tall, handsome fifteen-year-old boy with delicate facial features. A father and son. The boy's right leg was deformed and being corrected with special steal braces, he also had a thick soled orthopaedic boot. Dr Mengele saw in this crippled pair, father and son, a classic example of Jewish degeneracy. He immediately had the two taken out of the column and then summoned an SS non-commissioned officer. Having torn two sheets out of his notebook and jotted down a few words, he handed them to the SS-man with instructions escort both unfortunates to Crematorium I.

It was around twelve noon and Crematorium I was not working that day. There were no tasks for me either, so I was in my room and that is where the SS-man on duty found me. I was summoned to the gate. They were already standing there with their SS escort – the father and son. I was given the written instructions addressed to me. On the notepaper it said: 'Dissecting room, Crem. I. No.1 to clinically examine both cases. Exact measurements to be made of father and son. Fully detailed medical cards to be produced with special regard to possible causes of anomalies observed.'

The other letter was addressed to *Oberscharführer* Muhsfeldt. I didn't have to read to know what instructions it contained. I told one of the men on duty to hand it to Muhsfeldt.

The father and son – tragic figures from the Łódź Ghetto – looked at me silently, their hearts in their mouths. As I escorted them across the sun-drenched courtyard I started talking to them to make them feel more at ease. We entered the dissecting room. Thankfully, there was no corpse on the dissecting table – it would have been an extremely distressing sight. To spare them any other unpleasantness, I decided to examine them in the warm, sunlit surgery rather than the gloomy dissecting room, which stank of chemicals. From our conversation I found out that before the war the father had been a textiles wholesaler who also owned an emporium in Łódź and had travelled several times to Vienna hoping that renowned professors there would be able to cure his son.

First I carried out a thorough medical examination of the father. The lateral curvature of the spine and the resulting hunch had been caused by rachitis, more commonly known as rickets, which he had suffered relatively late in life. Despite a very meticulous examination, I couldn't find any symptoms of other diseases. I tried to put his mind at rest by assuring him they would most probably be sent to a labour camp.

I also conversed with the boy during his examination. He had an intelligent look but was quite distraught. With a frightened, quavering voice he related to me the countless horrors he had had to observe and personally experience during his five years in the Łódź Ghetto. He was barely ten when his family found itself within its walls. His mother, a frail and delicate woman, did not suffer long all the misfortunes the befell them. She succumbed to depression and melancholy, and for weeks would eat virtually nothing, so that her husband and child could have more. The totally devoted wife and dedicated mother died in the first year of their incarceration. The husband and son had to live on without her.

And now they were here in the crematorium. What a terrible irony of fate! It had befallen me, a Jewish doctor, to meticulously examine them before they died, and then I would have to dissect their still warm bodies. I was so sensitive to the immense tragedy of the situation and my own helplessness that it was almost driving me insane. Once again I was close to a nervous breakdown.

By whose will had our wretched people been made to suffer such a succession of horrors? If it was the will of God, I felt even He must be ashamed, for He couldn't have desired something as terrible as this.

I summoned up what strength I had left in me to examine the boy. I was able to confirm that the right leg had an inborn defect by which certain joints had failed to develop properly. The scientific name for this condition was hypomelia. More than once the hands of outstanding surgeons had operated on the leg. As a result it was now shorter, but with the help of bandages and the orthopaedic shoe the boy could still use it. I couldn't find any other defects.

I asked whether they would like something to eat. Both were very hungry, so I had some food to brought over. A while later they were ravenously consuming two large portions of beef stew with macaroni. You could only get such food in the *Sonderkommando*. They must have forgotten when they last ate anything like this. They didn't know it yet. I, on the other hand, was perfectly aware of the fact that this was their last meal.

Less than half an hour later *Oberscharführer* Muhsfeldt arrived together with four men from the *Sonderkommando*. They took the pair to the furnace room, where they were ordered to undress. Muhsfeldt fired two shots; the father and son collapsed on the bloodstained concrete floor. *Oberscharführer* Muhsfeldt had carried out Doctor Mengele's order.

Now it was once again my turn. The two corpses were carried into the dissecting room. I felt sick, and so asked my colleagues to perform the autopsies, while I typed the reports. The post-mortems revealed nothing that hadn't already been confirmed in the examinations carried out when the father and son were still alive. Nonetheless, these ordinary cases could, apparently, be used as scientific evidence of the degeneracy of Jews.

Doctor Mengele arrived in the evening – that day he has sent at least 10,000 people to their deaths. He listened with interest to my reports on both the *in vivo* and the post-mortem examinations of the unfortunate victims.

'These bodies cannot be burnt,' he said, 'Their skeletons must be conserved and sent to the Anthropological Museum in Berlin.'

He next asked me what I knew about cleaning skeletons. I replied that I knew of two methods. The first involved immersing the body for two weeks in a lime chloride solution, which burnt off the soft tissues surrounding the bones. Next the skeleton was immersed in petrol to remove the fat and whiten the bones. The second method was shorter. You simply boiled the corpse in water until the flesh easily came off the bone. Next you bathed the skeleton in petrol as in the first process.

Doctor Mengele ordered the shorter method of boiling to be applied. Concentration camp orders were always brief. The prisoner was not told how to carry out a given order and how to acquire the essential tools to realise it. An order was to be carried out, full stop! And now I found myself in exactly this kind of situation. I had been ordered to boil two corpses! Where? In what?

I turned to *Oberscharführer* Muhsfeldt for help. Even he was shocked to learn of the task I'd been given to do. He thought for a moment and then remembered that there were two empty iron barrels in the storeroom. He let me use them and suggested building a fireplace out of bricks in the courtyard, on top of which I could put the barrels with the corpses. I followed his advice. An improvised stove was built, the two barrels with their macabre contents were placed on top of it, and the process of cooking the corpses began. Two *Sonderkommando* men were employed to keep adding wood to the fire. After five hours and numerous tests I finally decided that the flesh had started separating from the bone. The fire was put out but the barrels were left outside to cool off.

I sat down in a shady spot nearby and start reading a book. It was quiet. The crematoria were not working that day. Instead four bricklayers from Auschwitz I were repairing the Crematorium I chimney.

It was almost dusk and assuming that the barrels had cooled down, I was about to get up, when suddenly one of the men posted to keep an eye on the barrels came running up to me, quite distraught, and shouted:

'Doctor! The Poles are eating the flesh in the barrels!'

I immediately got to my feet and rushed towards the fireplace. Four men in striped prison uniforms stood dumbstruck with horror by the barrels. They were the Polish bricklayers. They had finished their work and were waiting for an escort to take them back to the Auschwitz barracks. These hungry prisoners had decided to utilise this time by looking around for food and in this way they came across the two cauldrons, which had at that very moment been left unattended. They sniffed what was inside and assumed it to be boiled meat for the *Sonderkommando*. So they took out a few of the larger pieces, cut them up and proceeded to greedily devour them. Not for long, however, for the two *Sonderkommando* men soon returned and realised what was happening. When the bricklayers discovered what they had been eating they were transfixed, paralysed with terror.

Once the bones had been washed with petrol, our laboratory assistant very skilfully reassembled the skeletons. Both were laid on the table in the very same room where a day earlier I had examined the still living victims.

Doctor Mengele was very pleased. He invited several other doctors, all high-ranking officers, to see the skeletons. They touched various parts with an air of superiority and competed with one another in showing off their knowledge of professional terminology. They behaved as if the physical defects of the skeletons were an extraordinary scientific discovery. *Pseudowissenschaft*, pseudoscientific claptrap! There were no particular anomalies here! Hundreds of thousands of people all over the world had similar disorders. Any doctor, even one with a small number of patients. could come across such cases. Nazi propaganda would exploit even the tiniest detail for its purposes, even if it involved lying and cunningly giving things the appearance of scientific objectivity. And those who saw these propaganda exhibits would accept them for what they appeared to be, for most people lack the knowledge to be critical.

The skeletons and accompanying documentation were packed in tough paper sacks and posted to Berlin with a special stamp: 'Urgent: for the war effort.'

Once the skeletons were gone I felt extremely tired. The tragic events concerning the father and son in the hours shortly before and after their deaths were something that I found very difficult to bear...

A week had gone by and the liquidation of the Łódź Ghetto was over. The October sun was also gone, covered up by clouds bearing cold autumn rain. Mists and darkness shrouded the concentration camp barracks. So too a fog had descended on my past, whereas my future was getting ever darker. The cold and dampness of the rain that had been pouring for days penetrated your body to the bone – all contributing to make my sense of despair even greater. Wherever I went, wherever I looked, I saw electrified barbed wire. A constant reminder of the hopelessness, the pointlessness of life.

On the third day following the liquidation of the Łódź Ghetto the *Oberkapo* of the *Sonderkommando* brought a woman and two children, all soaked to the skin. Anticipating that something bad was going to happen, they had broken away from the rest of the transport and hidden behind some logs in the crematorium courtyard. They saw the entire transport descend into the ground and not one of them re-emerges. Shaking with terror they waited for a miracle to save them, but it didn't happen. They had endured three days out in the cold air and pouring rain in clothes that were completely drenched, without food, half conscious, until the *Oberkapo* finally came across them while finishing one of his patrols. Not knowing what to do, he took them to *Oberscharführer* Muhsfeldt. The woman, in her early thirties but looking more like fifty, just skin and bone, fell to her knees before the SS-man. With what strength there was left she hugged his boots, begging him with heart rendering tone of desperation to spare her and her children's lives. She said that for five years she had worked in a ghetto factory making uniforms for the German Army. She wanted to continue working if only they would spare their lives. But there was no mercy! They had to die!

And so they were killed. But his Auschwitz experiences must have affected the *Oberscharführer's* nerves, for he had someone else carry out the murders.

XXXI

We forgot about that bloody episode. We forgot because we had to, so that the many horrible experiences and the knowledge of the hopelessness of our own situation would not drive us insane. Luminal helped us considerably here.

I frequently looked back on the past, the pre-concentration camp days as if they were just a dream. Forget about everything, think of nothing, that was my only goal.

It was 1st November 1944: All Saints' Day. Large snowflakes were falling. The watchtowers were now barely visible. Everything was obscured by the white flakes. Only flocks of hungry crows rose up in the air from time to time, whenever the wind rattled the barbed-wire enclosure.

Despite the weather, at dusk I went for a short walk. I felt the cold air would refresh me and calm my frayed nerves. I strolled round the courtyard several times, and then approached the gas chamber. There I paused for a few seconds. I suddenly remembered it was All Souls' Day... All around me there was silence. The cold concrete steps leading down to the undressing room dissolved into darkness in the fading light. Millions of people had said goodbye to their lives at this threshold, before going to their deaths and later being even denied their own grave... I stood alone on this the last stage of so many people's lives. I felt the sad duty weighing down on me: to remember the souls in the name of their families scattered all over the world...

I left that sorrowful place and returned to my room. When I opened the door and I was surprised to see the room illuminated by flickering candle flames instead of an electric light bulb. My first thought was that the fuses had blown. Then I noticed my colleague, the associate professor from Szombathely University, sitting at the table, leaning on his elbows and staring fixedly at a flame. He hasn't even noticed my presence. The candlelight falling on his face made him look much older than he really was. I placed my hand on his shoulder and gently asked:

'Denes, why have you lit these candles?'

He mumbled something about both his in-laws, who had died fifteen years earlier. He did not mention his wife and child, who – and there were those in the *Sonderkommando* actually saw it – perished right here, in Crematorium I. I immediately recognised the symptoms of melancholic depression and reactionary amnesia, that is, the inability to recall certain experiences.

Putting my arm round him, I led him to his bed.

My poor friend! You were a doctor with immense knowledge, a slight body, quiet voice and a sensitive heart. Instead of curing the sick, you had fallen into a hell-hole of death, inhabited it and for many months witnessed tragedies and horrors that surpassed human understanding, and which no human being living beyond that wretched place could ever believe.

Perhaps it was better that your nerves had failed you and your mind was now misted up. At least you wouldn't have to comprehend what was yet to come.

XXXII

After a few days' silence, the usual bustle returned to the crematorium. The engines were running again, driving huge ventilation fans that fed the flames in the ovens. We were told to prepare for the arrival of transports from Terezin.

Terezin[54] used to be a garrison town in Czechoslovakia. The Germans changed its character by removing the garrison, deporting the civilian population and converting the town into a 'showpiece ghetto'. Its new inhabitants became Jews brought in from Czechoslovakia, Austria and Holland. Approximately 70,000 in all. Living conditions there were relatively good. The inhabitants were allowed to continue their trades as well as receive letters and Red Cross parcels. Red Cross representatives from neutral countries actually visited the ghetto on several occasions, and after each visit they gave positive reports on the situation there. Thus the Germans achieved their objective, for the 'showpiece ghetto' had been set up for the purpose of countering and disproving all news of the horrors of the concentration camps and crematoria, so that such news could be treated as libel and slander.

However, on the eve of its collapse, the Third Reich had ceased caring about world opinion and cast aside its mask. The relentless extermination of all remaining Jews had begun. And so it was now the turn of the Terezin ghetto.

Reich Central Security Office
Forced Labour Department

Summons
Jew .... of the Reich Protectorate is hereby informed
that by the ruling of the above authorities he is summoned to do
forced labour. The summoned Jew is hereby obliged to report to
the said authorities, and then to prepare the tools necessary to
carry out his trade, warm clothes, bed sheets and enough food for
a one-week journey. The date of departure will be publicly an-
nounced.
Terezin ....

Signature

It was with such documents that still able-bodied men from the Terezin ghetto arrived at the Auschwitz crematorium. The summons to do forced labour was a vile trick used to facilitate the process of extermination as well as acquire work tools and warm, winter clothes.

Two thousand fit young men perished in the gas chambers and their bodies were turned into ash in the crematorium fire. The exterminations lasted two days, then the crematoria fell silent.

Fourteen days later long trains started pulling up along the Jewish ramp once more, and this time women and children emerged from the boxcars. There was no selection, they all went to the left.

Hundreds of pieces of paper littered the undressing room floor. They read as follows:

Reich Central Security Office
Forced Labour Department

Summons

*The above authorities allow the wife and children of Jew
.... of the Reich Protectorate, who has been called on to do
forced labour, to travel to the above named Jew's place of work
for the purpose of living together. All those leaving are assured
suitable lodgings. The travellers are advised to take warm
clothes, bed sheets and enough food for a one-week journey.
Terezin ....*

Signature

Thousands of wives wishing to ease their husbands' burden
and thousands of children missing their fathers followed the twenty
thousand men to their deaths. That was the effect of this diabolical summons.

XXXIII

In the early morning of 17th November 1944[55] an SS non-commissioned officer entered my room to confidentially inform me that the Führer had categorically forbidden any further killing of people by any means on concentration camp territory. Having witnessed so much deception in the past, I could not accept this news at face value. Nor did conceal my scepticism from the bearer of the good news, but he insisted that this was an actual order that had been transmitted in a radio message to the crematorium and *Politische Abteilung*. Time would tell. Though I still felt fairly certain that it was yet another trick.

However, later that same morning I discovered that the news was indeed true. A train, five boxcars long, delivering five hundred sick and emaciated prisoners to 'a rest camp' ground to a halt on the railway tracks between crematoria I and II. I witnessed how one of the SS commissions approached and spoke the commander of the escort detachment. The outcome of their conversation was that the train moved in the reverse direction away from the crematorium gates, and the prisoners were later put in the hospital barracks of section F [BIIf]. That was the first time since I had arrived at the crematorium that a transport of prisoners who had been sent there to 'recuperate' were not lying an hour later with smashed skulls on a blood-drenched concrete floor in front of the ovens, but were instead actually lying in hospital beds and receiving medical care.

Less than hour later a new transport arrived. Five hundred Jews from Slovakia: the old, the young, men, women and children. I waited on tenterhooks to see what would happen next. The usual routine on the Jewish ramp was for the prisoners to be assembled and undergo selection. This time I observed something quite extraordinary. The weary travellers got out of the boxcars, but whereas normally they would have had to leave their larger luggage behind, this time they were taking all of it with them and going straight to the right side of the platform. They moved off to section E [BIIe}; mothers pushing prams with their infants inside, the young helping the sick and old. With an uplifted heart I registered another fact verifying the good news. It was now beyond doubt: this time the crematorium gates did not open to accept transports of prisoners designated for extermination. This was, indeed, good news for concentration camp prisoners, and yet simultaneously it foretokened liquidation of the *Sonderkommando*.

I was now certain they would do away with us even before the customary four months were up. There was new life emerging in the camp: they had now stopped the mass killings of prisoners, but at the same time they would have to cover up the bloody past. The crematoria would have to be dismantled, the burning ditches filled up and all the witnesses of those heinous crimes, killed. We greeted the imminence of death with solemn calmness and yet simultaneously with great joy at this turn of events. It was late in the day but, nonetheless, several thousand people were still alive of the six million sent by order of the demented Führer, the pyromaniac of the Third Reich, to Majdanek, Treblinka, Auschwitz and Birkenau to be exterminated.

At around noon I apprehensively searched for the SS radio operator who had brought me the good news in the morning. I wanted to know if there had been any further messages since then, and if perchance there were some special instructions concerning the *Sonderkommando*. To my relief, I found him alone in his room. In reply to my question he said: 'In a few days time the *Sonder-*

kommando is to be sent to do hard labour in one of the underground plants near Breslau.' I didn't believe a single word of it, but I also knew he didn't want to deceive me out of malice, he was lying out of pity. Perhaps because I had once cured him of a serious disease.

XXXIV

By my watch it was two in the afternoon. We were having lunch and I was vacantly observing the snow-bearing clouds from the window of my room. Suddenly a sonorous voice interrupted the silence in the corridor.

'*Alle antreten*! (Everyone out!)'

We heard such yelling every morning and evening for roll call, yet in the afternoon it took on a very sinister meaning.

'*Antreten! Alle antreten!*' we heard repeated in an ever harsher tone. Soon there was the sound of heavy footsteps approaching our door. It was flung open and an SS-man yelled: '*Antreten!*'

So the time had come. We went out into the courtyard. The unit of SS guards was waiting for us in a state of full readiness. Our companions were already there. There was no expression of surprise on their faces. They were silent. The extended line of SS-men with their sub-machineguns levelled at us was silent too. They were patiently waiting for the whole *Sonderkommando* to gather. I looked round. The nearby copse of pines was already half buried in snow. There was silence everywhere.

After a few minutes the command was given: 'To the left, turn!' We proceeded past the dense rank of armed guards. On leaving the courtyard we did not go out onto the road, instead we headed for Crematorium II. We crossed its courtyard fully understanding that this was our last journey. They led us to the furnace room. None of the SS-men stayed inside. Instead they surrounded the building, aiming their guns at every window and door,

152

ready to shoot, though the doors were locked and the windows barred. It was impossible to get out.

Our companions from Crematorium II were already inside. Soon we were joined by the men from Crematorium IV. All in all, there were 460 of us.[56] We were awaiting death and wondering how they were going to do it. We were all experts by then and knew the various methods of extermination used by the SS. The gas chamber? That was infeasible as far as the *Sonderkommando* was concerned. Shooting? Impracticable inside a building. The most likely option would be to blow the whole crematorium up and us with it, thus killing two birds with one stone. A feat worthy of the SS. Or perhaps they'd toss in a few phosphorous grenades? Apparently that was what they had done to the inhabitants of Milo after they had been packed into boxcars. They were all dead even before the transport moved. Only corpses arrived at the Auschwitz crematorium.

The *Kommando* sat on the concrete floor in the furnace room in silence. If anyone said anything, it was in a quiet whisper. Suddenly a tall, slim, dark-haired man in his early thirties got up. In a loud voice, so that everyone could hear, he started to speak. It was Dajan – a Rabbi's assistant from some small religious community in Poland. A self-taught man of great religious learning, enlightenment and also an ascetic. Even here, in the *Sonderkommando*, he had followed his austere religious principles and, despite the well-stocked larder, restricted his diet to bread, margarine and onions. He had been assigned the job of a stoker, but I managed to persuade *Oberscharführer* Muhsfeldt to relieve this fanatical believer from having to perform such a ghastly task. I put forward the following arguments: 'This job requires physical strength, something Dajan does not posses, because his ascetic code of conduct means that he hardly eats anything and is now quite weak. Besides there are other reasons why he is unsuitable for this work. He would only get in the way of the others by having utter prayers for each body thrown into the fire, and that would be several thousand times a day.' I could not think of any other reasons, but the *Oberscharführer* agreed to have Dajan reassigned to work at the rubbish tip in the Crematorium II courtyard. It needs to be explained that this rubbish tip was where all the used--up items and decaying food off the transports was collected. This also included documents, diplomas, army certificates, passports, photographs, prayer books, prayer latchets, talliths and various other Jewish religious artefacts that had been brought to Auschwitz by those going to the gas chambers. The SS regarded all this as rubbish only fit to be burnt. Needless to say, the rubbish tip was kept constantly ablaze. The fire consumed hundreds of thousands of family photographs, of parents, beautiful girls and beloved children as well as thousands of prayer books. Many a time I had held in my hands those photographs and prayer books. Virtually every prayer book contained annotations recording the dates of parents' deaths and carefully pressed flowers, no doubt picked from family graves that were to be found in every part of Europe. All this was added to the heap, together with the expensive and ordinary talliths and other religious artefacts, and burnt.

This was where Dajan worked, or rather didn't work, he just looked at the flames. When I asked him how he felt, he said that he was unhappy. The burning of prayer books, talliths, prayer latchets and other religious objects was also a very upsetting task. I felt genuinely sorry for him, but I couldn't find him any other job. This was after all a *Sonderkommando* whose purpose it was to work in the crematorium.

That was the Dajan who had just got up and started to speak: "Fellow Jews... An inscrutable Will has sent our people to its death; fate has allotted us the cruellest of tasks, that of participating in our own destruction, of witnessing our own disappearance, down to the very ashes to which we are reduced. In no instance have the heavens opened to send showers and put out the funeral pyre flames. We must accept, resignedly, as Sons of Israel should, that this is the way things must be. God has so ordained it. Why? It is not for us, miserable humans, to seek the answer. This is the fate that has befallen us. Do not be afraid of death. What is life worth, even if, by some strange miracle, we should manage to remain alive? We would return to our cities and towns to find cold and pillaged homes. In every room, in every corner, the memory of those who have disappeared would lurk, haunting our tear-filled eyes. Stripped of family and relatives, we would wander like the restless, shuffling shadows of our former selves, of our completed pasts, finding nowhere any peace or rest".

His eyes were bright and his gaunt face looked inspired. The rest of the room was silent. Only from time to time was there the sound of a match being struck as someone lit a cigarette, or someone else gave a heavy sigh. The living were saying farewell to the dead.

Then all of a sudden the huge door opened and *Oberscharführer* Steinberg entered accompanied by two guards armed with sub-machineguns.

'*Ärzte heraus!*' he yelled impatiently.

I left the chamber together with my two colleagues and the laboratory assistant. Halfway on the road back to Crematorium I Steinberg and the guards stopped. The *Oberscharführer* handed me a sheet of paper with numbers on it and told me to cross out mine. This was list of *Sonderkommando* camp numbers. In a short while I found the number that was tattooed on my arm, A 8450, and deleted it with an indelible pen. Steinberg also ordered me to delete the numbers of my companions. Then they escorted us the rest of the way to the crematorium, where we were instructed to go to our room and stay there.

The next day a column of five lorries pulled up in the crematorium courtyard, and the bodies of the *Sonderkommando* prisoners were thrown out. Thirty newly recruited prisoners carried the bodies into the furnace room. There were terrible burns on the corpses. Their clothes were in tatters and the faces were scorched beyond recognition. It was impossible to identify who they were. In most cases even the tattooed numbers were gone.

After the gassings, after the pyres, the lethal chloroform injections into the heart, the shootings in the back of the head, the phosphorous grenades, I now discovered a sixth method of murder. The previous night our unfortunate companions had been taken into the forest and exterminated with flame-throwers[57].

Only we four remained. And once again it had nothing to do with any consideration for us, any personal wish to spare our lives. We were simply needed to carry out some work. There was no reason to be pleased, no sense of relief. Dr Mengele had simply granted us another temporary reprieve.

XXXV

The extermination of the Thirteenth Sonderkommando was now another episode recorded in the crematoria's bloody history.

We wandered aimlessly in between the cold chamber walls, unable to find space for ourselves. In the dead silence the echoing of our footsteps was literally ringing in my ears. There was nothing to do. The days passed in idleness, the nights in vigilant anticipation. Only we four remained in the building. The thirty new prisoners could hardly be considered a *Sonderkommando*: they lived in the camp and came every other day to burn the bodies of those who had died in the camp hospitals.

We felt dejected, broken by the constant waiting for the end to come. *Oberscharführer* Muhsfeldt had changed, he now avoided having any contact with us. That was a bad sign. It meant he also felt that he outlived his usefulness. The end to the tragedy was fast approaching and now it was time for those who knew the dark secrets. He sat in his room for days on end, drinking heavily in order forget about his criminal past and not to think about what the future held for him.

Then one day, quite unexpectedly, Dr Mengele arrived. He found us immediately, for he knew perfectly well that we hadn't been given any work for some time. He informed us that Auschwitz concentration camp was to be liquidated. This time it was not the prisoners who were to be liquidated but the actual camp itself. Two of the existing crematoria were to be dismantled, the third was to continue burning the bodies of prisoners who had died in the camp. We four, together with all our dissecting room equipment, museum pieces and archives, were to be moved to Crematorium IV – the one that was to remain active. So it was crematoria I and II which were to be immediately demolished. As we know, Crematorium III had been burnt down during the *Sonderkommando* revolt of 6th October[58].

This was indeed a historic moment when the following day thousands of prisoners filled the Crematorium I courtyard and, having been divided into smaller squads, proceeded to dismantle this building with its terrible, bloody past.

Our hearts filled with joy when the dynamite charges exploded, turning one by one the redbrick walls into rumble and dust, and thus heralding the fall of the Third Reich. Jews had built that edifice and now they were pulling it down. Looking at their faces I saw that they were working with determination, as no concentration camp inmate had ever worked before. They were now working with the hope that better days lay ahead...

We packed everything that could be taken from the dissecting room and laboratory. We took only the marble top from the dissecting table: a new concrete base would have to be made in Crematorium IV. The move lasted several hours. We spent the night in our new home.

The dissecting table and the various racks were set up, the museum pieces were put in place, and soon the new dissecting room and laboratory were ready.

And once again nothing happened for days on end. The idleness made us apathetic. We wandered round the crematorium aimlessly. Our SS overseers had totally succumbed to alcohol, their only means of escape. They were now hardly ever sober.

One evening, while we are having supper, *Oberscharführer* Muhsfeldt staggered into our room. He leant over our table and in a drunken slur declared:

'Evening, boys! Soon you'll all be dead, but then it'll be our turn!'

The inebriated Muhsfeldt's words confirmed my assumption: our persecutors and executioners were to perish with us.

I offered the SS-man hot tea laced with rum. He clearly liked it and later kept refilling his glass. He seated himself at our table and started talking, as if to make up for lost time. He told us about his wife, who had died in a bombing raid, and his son, who had fallen on the Russian Front.

'It's over!' he declared. 'The Russians are 40 kilometres from Auschwitz. The whole of Germany is on the roads. Everyone wants to get away from the border areas.'

The SS-man's words awakened in me a glimmer of hope. 'Perhaps, despite everything, we might just survive...?'

XXXVI

We greeted 1st January 1945 with a mixture of hope and apprehension.

The morning of New Year's Day. There was snow as far as the eye could see. Everything was white. I went out for a short stroll round the crematorium courtyard. The silence was broken by the sound of an engine. In a few moments a very large brown van entered the crematorium courtyard. It was a van for transporting concentration camp prisoners, who called it 'Brown Toni'.

A high-ranking SS officer got out of the driver's cabin. I recognised him and gave the regulation salute. It was Dr Klein, an SS physician and *Sturmbannführer*[59], one of the bloody butchers of Auschwitz. Block 11 was the camp gaol. That was from where a hundred new victims had now been delivered.

'I've brought you some work for the New Year,' he said to the *Oberscharführer* hurrying towards him. Muhsfeldt was so drunk that he could barely stand. He had really raised the roof on New Year's Eve. Perhaps in a strange way he was already holding his own wake. The grimace on his face showed that he was displeased with having to perform that bloody task on New Year's Day.

A hundred Poles had arrived here to die. SS guards led them to a chamber beside the furnace room. From inside an order was yelled: 'Undress at once!' Meanwhile Dr Klein strolled round the courtyard accompanied by Muhsfeldt. I quickly went into the building to talk to the condemned prisoners.

160

One of them, a man from Krakow, told me that one night he had given shelter to a relative at his home. The Gestapo had charged him with harbouring partisans and put him before a court martial. He had been awaiting his sentence in Block 11 and assumed that they had been brought here to be bathed, after which all of them would be sent to do hard labour. The poor man did not realise that the mere fact that he was in that particular building meant that he had been sentenced to death! He didn't know this because no one had told him.

Another condemned man was sent to prison for raising prices: he had bought half a kilogram of butter without a ration card. That was his only crime. A third man inadvertently wandered into a security zone: he was accused of being a partisan and spy. And all the other men in turn had similar stories to tell. Minor transgressions and unsubstantiated suspicions.

There was no Sonderkommando now, so SS-men had to lead the victims to Muhsfeldt.

Once again the roar of the engine: 'Brown Toni' had returned with new victims. This time a hundred elegantly dressed women emerged from the lorry. They were all Polish, and they too went the that room and were ordered to undress. Then one by one they were led away to be shot. They paid with their lives for the tiniest of transgressions.

The SS-men next proceeded to burn the bodies. They came to me asking for some rubber gloves, which they needed to carry out the job. Having confirmed that all 200 victims were dead, Dr Klein left.

According to the SS-men, there was no contradiction between the decree of 17th November suspending all killings and that day's executions. That day they were merely carrying out court-martial sentences[60]. This was mass murder once again, but in keeping with the law!

XXXVII

Nothing had been happening for some time now. The days passed by monotonously. The only news was that Dr Mengele had left. The concentration camp had a new chief physician. In fact it was no longer a concentration camp but a labour camp. With the New Year the *Konzentrationslager* was officially reclassified as an *Arbeitslager*[61]. Everything was falling apart.

On 10th January I acquired a newspaper from which I learnt that the Russian offensive had begun. The windowpanes in my room now trembled from the sound of distant detonations. The front was getting ever closer.

January 17th, although I wasn't tired, I went to bed early and soon fell asleep in the pleasant warmth given out by a coke stove. It must have been around midnight when I was suddenly awoken by loud explosions, the sound of machinegun fire and blinding flashes of light.

I heard doors slamming and heavy footsteps fading away down the corridor. I jumped out of bed, eager to find out what was happening. Opening the door to the corridor, I saw that furnace room lights were on and the doors to the SS-men's quarters wide open. All this suggested that the guards had fled.

The heavy oak crematorium door was also open. There was no guard in sight. My eyes immediately turned to the watchtower. For the first time in eight months I saw them empty!

I rushed back to our room, woke my companions and started dressing. We were preparing to leave! The SS had fled. We could not afford to stay a while longer in that place where for the last eight months we had been threatened with death every day, every hour. We couldn't wait there for the Russians because we couldn't be sure that no SS rearguard would enter the camp. If they did and found us here, they would certainly shoot us on the spot!

We were dressed. We'd put on plenty of good quality, warm clothes, jumpers, winter coats and, what was most essential in an −18° C frost, some good boots. Each of us also took one kilo of tinned meat and stuffed our pockets with medicines and cigarettes.

We were now ready to leave; there was the euphoric feeling of regained freedom. The direction we headed for was the Birkenau camp! It lay two kilometres from the crematorium[62]. There was a glow on the horizon. It was probably the camp burning.

We ran through the furnace room and passed the open door of the treasury. There was gold still lying in boxes that had been ripped open by the fleeing SS. They could only have taken a small proportion of the loot. The thought of taking anything from there didn't even enter our heads. We were running for our lives and knew all too well the merely relative value of such treasures. Only one thing was important to us: freedom!

We went through the gate. No one stopped us. This was an unbelievable turn of events. We made our way through the snow-covered Brzezinka grove. The same path down which millions had gone to their death. We passed the tracks and the Jewish ramp, all beneath a blanket of snow. Here millions of victims had clambered out of the boxcars. Here all the farewells had been said between those selected to go to the left and those selected to join the right-hand column. It was just a matter of time, of course, when these people died – ultimately they were all meant to die...

Yes, it was Birkenau burning![63] The guardhouses and the offices with all the camp records were ablaze[64]. In front of the main gate stood a dark mass of people. These were columns of prisoners waiting for the order to march. There must have been about 3,000 of them[65]. Without much hesitation we decided to join them. I considered this to be the best solution, and my colleagues agreed. No one would spot us in the crowd. We were no longer members of the *Sonderkommando*! We were no longer the officially known holders of the Third Reich's criminal secrets, so the death sentence was no longer hanging over us. We were ordinary prisoners marching in a large column.

Everyone was fleeing. They couldn't drive us on for long! In two, three day's time the Russians would have caught up. Then the SS were bound to leave us somewhere on the way. In a situation when the front line was in such a fluid state it was best to keep with the other prisoners.

It was around one in the morning. The last SS-man left the camp. They switched off all the lights in camp from the guardhouse by the main gate. The gates were closed for the last time and darkness descended on Birkenau, which now became a huge cemetery of European nations. I gazed once more at the complex of barracks and barbed wire. This was my farewell to the grave of millions.

We were surrounded by an SS detachment and then the marching began. We were soon discussing the day's events with our new companions. We tried to guess what the next day held in store for us. Would the SS escort succeed in getting us to the intended destination or would they abandon us somewhere on the way?

We had barely gone five kilometres when the left side of our column was subjected to deadly machinegun fire. A Russian advance guard had caught up with us. Mistaking our column for German troops, they attacked with several machineguns and a light tank. The SS ordered us to lie down on the ground and returned fire. A ferocious gun battle ensued[66]. Then there was silence.

It was now growing light. During the night we had covered a distance of 15 kilometres. The snow on the road had already been packed beneath the feet of those who had gone before us. Bowls, blankets and wooden clogs lay scattered everywhere.

A column of women prisoners must have gone down this route; we could tell by the discarded objects.

A few kilometres on we learnt more about this column: every 40 or 50 metres, we saw women's corpses lying in the roadside ditch, their faces covered in blood. And so it continued for the rest of the way. Corpses, corpses, corpses. Every fifty paces, corpses! They had no longer had the physical strength to go on, and whoever lagged behind, got shot. So the SS had been instructed not leave anyone alive! This was not comforting news. We were shocked by this never-ending trail of corpses. We tried to go faster. We were marching for our lives!

Then we heard the first shots in our column. Two of our companions remained on the wayside. They had been unable to go on and sat down, so they were shot. Soon we heard gunfire every few minutes.

We reached Pszczyna at noon. This was the first respite in out journey. We spent an hour on a football pitch. Those who had anything to eat now tried to satisfy their hunger. We each smoked a cigarette and with renewed strength set off down the snow-
-covered road.

The march lasted five days before we finally reached the railway station in Wodzisław. Without food or water, sleeping out in the open, we had covered a distance of over 60 kilometres. The column had been reduced to 2,000 prisoners by the time we got to the station. Approximately 600 men were shot on the way. It was a great relief to see a train of open coal trucks waiting for us alongside the platform.

We were quickly loaded into the trucks, but had to wait the whole night before the transport moved. I didn't count how many unfortunate companions froze to death during the five-day journey, but when we finally reached Mauthausen concentration camp there were only 1,500 of us left. Among the 500 who didn't complete the journey there must have also been those who had found an opportune moment to escape.

XXXVIII

The gloomy granite walls of Mauthausen concentration camp were perched on a hilltop above the town with the same name like an ancient castle. That was our destination. This extermination camp had been built out of hundreds of thousands of granite blocks. Even from afar, the tall turrets and artillery muzzles jutting out of openings in walls revealed the characteristics of a fortress. Were the stones covered with the patina of time, this would undoubtedly have made a picturesque image. However, the glaring whiteness of the fortress clashed with the dark forests surrounding it. The stones were still white because the castle had only recently been built. The Third Reich decided to have a concentration camp built there, so after the defeat of France thousands of former fighters for the freedom of Spain and hundreds of thousands of German Jews were brought to this place. They were made to work in the Mauthausen stone quarries. They were made to cut out granite blocks and carry them up the rocky mountain road leading to the camp. They were the ones who had to raise the granite walls surrounding their wretched barracks. Though all were already condemned to death, they first had to raise this place of torture and execution, and suffer unimaginable pain. And only then did they all perish.

Since then, of course, the camp was never empty. Thousands of Yugoslav fighters were brought here, resistance fighters from all of occupied Europe, tens of thousands of condemned Jews. The barracks were sometimes empty, but never for more than a few days before being filled again with more prisoners awaiting their turn to die.

Our transport, exhausted by the marching and chilled through to the bone, now slowly made it way up the long, snow-packed road. With what little strength their was left in our bodies we crossed the concentration camp gate and in the evening twilight assembled in the *Appelplatz*.

I looked for my companions. Laboratory assistant Fischer, our helper from the dissecting room, was missing. I last saw him in Pszczyna, lying on the snow. The altered features of his face were a sign of approaching death. He was fifty years old and had spent the last five in a concentration camp. His body was clearly unable cope with the long march and the freezing cold.

The young physician from Nice, Dr Körner, was totally exhausted, but he had every chance of recovering. Associate Professor Denes Görög, on the other hand, was now in the final stage of his illness. His spates of delirium were much more apparent than they had been at the crematorium, and even then hiding the disease was already becoming a problem. I had done everything I could to avoid any contact between him and Dr Mengele. Muhsfeldt was also a good observer, so I had to keep the poor man isolated from his potential executioner. He would not have survived a single minute if they had found out about his condition. He was aware of this fact, and when we were still at the crematorium he passed on to me his final will.

'Miklós,' he said, 'what with your willpower, you are bound to find your way home. However, I feel I will not live to see freedom again. My wife and daughter have perished here in the gas chamber. I know this fact for certain, because I have checked it myself. But I have managed to hide my son in a monastery at Köszeg. His name is Sandor and he is twelve. Adopt him if you manage to survive and return home. I am quite certain that soon I'll be dead. This is my last request.'

I promised Denes that I would fulfil his wish.

Fortunately our situation had changed, we were now far from the place where we could only expect death. But then again, now, at the end of this long journey, on the eve of liberation, when it seemed we could once more look to the future with hope, despite everything, the time had come to die! This was a real tragedy! After roll call we were all driven down a narrow passage leading to the bathhouse. We were joined by prisoners from various other camps. They, too, were waiting to go into the bathhouse. Probably some ten thousand people had been crammed in here. There was a bitterly cold wind blowing. We were on top of a foothill of the Alps, and winters could be very harsh there. They were letting 40 people into the bathhouse at time. That was how many they could fit in one go. After some quick mental arithmetic, I realised that it would take three days for everyone to get their turn! *Reichsdeutsche* criminals who were employed at the camp as the fire brigade were also the SS's most loyal lackeys. And it was they who were now in charge of keeping order among the other prisoners and letting them into the bathhouse. They were letting the Aryans through first. The rest could have to wait for up to three days, and getting into the bathhouse after such a long journey was matter of life and death. Only after the bathhouse did a prisoner get assigned to a barracks and put on the list of those to be fed. So before a prisoner reached the bathhouse, he had to stand outside in the freezing cold, hungry, exhausted and suffering from exposure after the murderous ten-day journey. He would have to wait for as long as his legs would support him and his eyes stayed open. And once his strength failed him, he'd lie down on the snow and never get up. Around me over 300 prisoners were already lying on the snow, having fallen asleep forever. No one took any notice of them. Here everyone was now fighting only for his own survival and the battle was reaching its climax.

Poor Denes had lost his glasses and was now drifting aimlessly in the crowd with his head uncovered, continually muttering strange words without any sense. I took him by the arm and started pulling him towards the bathhouse; perhaps we'd somehow manage to get the hot bath, which in this situation meant life. However, we did not get far before the crowd separated us and I lost sight of Denes. I called out his name, but to no avail. In the howling wind I could barely hear my own voice.

The danger was becoming more and more apparent. Summoning up all the strength that was left in me, I forced my way through the crowd towards the bathhouse. At last, I was in the front rows. Several SS-men and guards with thick rubber truncheons were standing in front of a group of prisoners. The prisoners were the next batch of 40 due to be let into the bathhouse. They were all Aryans. My instinct of self-preservation told me to break out of the crowd. I approached an *Oberscharführer* and in a resolute voice declared:

'*Herr Oberscharführer*! I am the physician of the transport from Auschwitz, please let me into bathhouse.'

The SS-man looked at me. Perhaps it was my clothes and purposeful manner that impressed him, or maybe my fluent German. I don't know. But he turned to a guard standing on the bathhouse steps and called: 'Let the doctor in!'

I was saved! Within a few minutes the hot water returned the sense of touch to my numb limbs. For the first time after ten days of freezing hell I found myself in a warm place. The hot water soothed my body and nerves. I was becoming my former self again.

Our clothes were considered to be contaminated and remained in the undressing room. I was sorry to have to part with my warm coat, suit and jumper, but at least they had left me my boots. A good pair of boots in a concentration camp was half the secret to staying alive. I put them on and together with the other newly washed prisoners left the bathhouse, naked. We had to wait for the next group to finish bathing, so that there was the required number of prisoners for a single barracks. Standing naked after a hot bath for half an hour in −18°C temperatures and icy winds can be a recipe for death.

At last the other 40-man group joined us and we started moving. Our SS escort ordered us to run. Five hundred metres on, we finally reached Barracks 23 of the quarantine camp. At the entrance to the barracks stood a thug wearing a green triangular badge: he was the block overseer. As the prisoners entered he handed each a quarter of a loaf of bread. The block clerk standing beside him then slapped onto the bread a heaped tablespoon of some meat substance from a tin and poured about a quarter of a litre of hot black coffee into each prisoner's canteen.

After ten days' fasting this was a feast fit for kings! Within a few seconds I had eaten everything and, in a blissful state, started looking round for a place to rest. I found it in a corner of the barracks. Corners had the advantage that other prisoners didn't walk back and forth over you when you were trying to sleep. Of course, we had to sleep on the floor: there were no bunks in quarantine barracks. Despite this, I slept soundly until reveille. On waking the first thing I thought of were my friends, who were still waiting for their bath, that was, if they were still alive.

We spent three days sitting on the floor or wandering round the barracks. The food we received was bearable and we had some form of respite after the arduous journey.

On the third day an SS officer entered the barracks accompanied by someone from the camp office and summoned all those who had worked in the Auschwitz crematoria to come forward. Could they have had a list? With their fiendishly efficient organisation it seemed quite plausible. But then I realised it was just a ploy. They wanted to find those who knew the secrets of the Auschwitz crematoria, but if they had had a list, they would have simply read out the camp numbers. From this I could deduce that did not yet know who I was. There followed a long tense moment of silence. Then the SS officer left. I'd won! I had won life, and not for the first time.

That evening we received our striped uniforms and headed down to the station in Mauthausen town. Seven hundred prisoners were put on a train bound for a concentration camp in Melk on the Danube. This time, however, we were in closed carriages and able to sit on benches. The journey lasted only three hours.

The camp at Melk was also situated on a hill. The buildings had once been army engineers' barracks. These huge structures, surrounded by a wall, housed 15,000 prisoners. Our difficult situation was made a little easier to bear because of the beautiful surroundings. There was a splendid baroque abbey on a rocky hill above us, and below us in the valley, the winding Danube, the river of our fatherland. It was possible to imagine that we were at home...

XXXIX

Spring came early in 1945.

It was the beginning of April, and beyond the barbed-wire enclosure of the concentration camp at Melk the trees were starting to turn green. There were still some patches of snow on the banks of the Danube below us, but the green grass was gradually taking over. I had experienced eight weeks of both good and bad days in yet another concentration camp. I was now tired and weak. Only the hope of imminent liberation prevented me from succumbing to melancholy.

And here too everything was falling apart. The Third of Reich was in its death throes before my very eyes. Never-ending columns of defeated armies were retreating deep into the interior of Germany, which had by now been reduced into a smouldering ruin. Hundreds of riverboats and barges carried the populations of evacuated cities upstream on the swelled vernal waters of the Danube.

Nothing lasts forever... The dream of a millennial Third Reich had suddenly evaporated. The belief in the supremacy of a Germanic race that was destined to rule the world was now being dispelled and replaced by bitter disillusionment. The peoples of Europe now anticipating liberation were no longer in mortal danger; their towns would longer be ransacked nor their capitals 'erased' from the map of Europe. They wouldn't have numbers branded on their arms; they wouldn't be deported from their homes and turned into galley slaves guarded by men in death's head SS caps and specially trained dogs. The Third Reich was now departing from the world stage. Like a pyromaniac it had wished to set the world ablaze, only to ultimately perish in its own fire. The corporal's rasping voice announcing to the world through the ether, '*Deutschland über alles*!' was now almost silent. Freedom loving nations had broken the arrogance of the Third Reich and now life was taking a new course.

On 7th April 1945 the arc lights on the perimeter posts of the Melk concentration camp went out. Darkness and silence had now also descended on this place, too. Everyone left and the gates were closed. Seven thousand prisoners were taken even deeper into the German interior. First they put us on river boats and later marched us along roads that were packed with refugees. For seven days we proceeded up snow-covered, mountain ridge tracks before we finally reached our new destination.

The concentration camp at Ebensee was the fourth one I was forced to enter. Here too the first item on the agenda was a roll call lasting for hours on end. Second: the bathhouse. Third: quarantine in a foul barracks run by thugs with rubber truncheons. I participated in all three items of this programme. I was first frozen stiff by the icy wind and then the cold rain seeped in through my flimsy uniform during interminable roll calls.

Bitterness was raging within me. It could only be a matter of days before liberation came, yet we awaited for events to unfold with a degree of apprehension. After all, for us it could all end in a blood-bath. Before the liberators came, we could all be exterminated. Having survived 12 months of concentration camps and lawlessness, it would be an end to our vicissitudes in typical Third Reich style.

But it was not to be!

On 5th May 1945 a white flag was hoisted on a watchtower at Ebensee. It shone brightly in the spring sunlight. It was over! The Germans had laid down their arms! At around nine a small American tank arrived and three soldiers emerged from it to take over the camp.

We were free...

EPILOGUE

New found freedom put us, those who had been put beyond the law, on our feet. We left the barbed-wire enclosure and a vast expanse opened up before us. We summoned up what strength there was left within us. Sick, with broken body and soul, I set off on my homeward journey. It was not made any easier by the sight of the towns that I passed. Instead of flourishing with life, everywhere there were charred ruins and mass graves. I dreaded the thought of what lay ahead of me; my home in ruins and neither my parents nor my darling wife, daughter or sister there to greet me ever again.

The humiliations and sorrows, the horror of the crematoria and burning ditches, the eight months spent with the living dead of the *Sonderkommando* had all dulled sense of good and evil. I needed to rest. Recuperate. But for what purpose...? I was ill. The bloody past was taking its toll on my sick heart. My eyes had seen hundreds of thousands of people enter the gas chambers. I had seen people being burnt on pyres. On the orders of a fanatic regarding himself to be a genius, I had had to open up the corpses of hundreds of victims. I had worked for a man who was willing to exploit the death of millions of victims for the purposes of some pseudoscientific, crackpot theory. I had had to cut out flesh from healthy young women, so that Dr Mengele could breed bacteria. I had bathed the bodies of cripples and dwarfs in calcium chloride solutions or boiled them in cauldrons, so that their skeletons could be displayed in Third Reich museums for future generations and to justify to them the necessity of exterminating the 'lower races'. I had faced death twice when standing before an SS execution squad. I had seen the bloody corpses of 300 of my companions and was now the only living witness. I had travelled hundreds of kilometres through the snow and biting frost in order to reach new concentration camps.

How long that journey had been, and now I couldn't find space for myself in my own home. I drifted aimlessly through the silent rooms. The memories of the bloodshed and deep despair of the past made the present sad, too. I wandered the streets, a shadow of my former self, only stirring for a moment when I thought I recognised a familiar face among the passers-by.

I suffered in silence, despondently counting the passing days and months. It was already October. Six months had gone by since I was liberated. On a cold autumn afternoon I sat at home hoping the warmth of the stove would help mitigate the pain. Suddenly the doorbell rang. The front door opened, and my wife and daughter appeared. They had been liberated from the notorious Bergen--Belsen extermination camp. That was where they had come from. And they were healthy. They didn't speak much, and yet the few words they uttered said almost all there was to say. Then they both bust into tears and continued weeping for many hours. But I understood everything. Who could understand them better than I?

At last my life has a purpose. I have someone to live for! I want to work again. It will be good to be useful, to help other people once more.

But I shall never cut dead bodies again. Nevermore...

THE LIFE OF DR MIKLÓS NYISZLI

Miklós Nyiszli was born on 17th July 1901 at a place called Somlyo (now Simleul Silvaniei) in Romania. There he spent four years in a primary school and eight in a secondary school. In 1920 he started studying medicine at the University of Cluj (Kolozsvar). After completing the first year he moved to Germany and studied medicine at the University of Kiel. He later continued these studies in Breslau (Wrocław), where he became a doctor of medicine in 1930. That same year he returned to Romania and settled in the town of Oradea together his wife Margareta, whom he married in 1927, and daughter Zsuzsana, b. 1929. In 1937, after several years spent practising his profession, Nyiszli and his family moved to the small town of Viseu de Sus, which became part of Hungary after that country's treaty with Romania in 1940.

After German forces entered Hungary on 19th March 1944, pressure was put on Sztójay's newly installed, pro-German government to prepare for the deportation of approximately 800,000 of the country's Jewish inhabitants. A schedule was planned, according to which from mid-May over 12,000 Jews were to leave Hungary every day (on average four trains, each carrying 3,000 people). Most transports were bound for KL Auschwitz. The most common route was via Kosice, Muszyna, Tarnów and Krakow. The Hungarian escort was replaced by German military police on the Slovak border.

Dr Nyiszli and his family were also included in this deportation programme. They were first interned at a place called Sapinta, and then at Gyula, before being put on an Auschwitz-bound train in the second half of May 1944. On the railway ramp at Birkenau, Dr Nyiszli together with his wife and daughter were among those selected to go to the camp. There he was given camp number A-8450. Thanks to his expert knowledge of forensic medicine, Dr Mengele employed him to dissect the bodies of twins and dwarfs who were the subjects of his experiments. Another of Dr Nyiszli's tasks included providing of medical care to the SS guards and the prisoners who operated the gas chambers and crematoria.

Being quartered in Crematorium I (II) at Birkenau, Dr Nyiszli had a rare insight into the camp's most closely kept secret: the mass murder of thousands of people in the gas chambers. He witnessed the mass extermination of several thousand Jews from the family camp that was shipped in from Terezin, and then the annihilation of the Gypsies from the Gypsy camp. Moreover, he witnessed the outbreak and suppression of Sonderkommando revolt, because of which he was very nearly killed himself. He also survived the evacuation of Auschwitz in January 1945, but was only freed when the Americans liberated the camp at Ebensee on 5th May 1945.

After returning to Romania, Nyiszli started working again as a physician. Several months later his wife and daughter returned, having been liberated from Bergen-Belsen. He gave evidence at the Nuremberg trial of IG Farbenindustrie.

In the last years of his life Miklós Nyiszli suffered from ill health. He died of heart attack on 5th May 1956. His daughter Zsuzsana died on 8th January 1983 and his wife Margareta on 5th September 1985, aged 84.

Miklós Nyiszli wrote his memoirs shortly after the war, and they were published for the first time, in Hungarian, in 1946. Since then they have been translated into many languages.

Franciszek Piper

NOTES

¹ Prisoner Miklós Nyiszli was appointed by SS Doctor Josef Mengele to carry out post-mortems of twins and dwarfs whom Mengele had subjected to medical experiments. He was also a physician of the SS-men and prisoners operating the gas chambers and crematoria. The latter could not to be treated at the sickbays and so called hospitals situated in various parts of the camp, for contact with other prisoners outside the *Sonderkommando* was strictly prohibited. This was an attempt to try to keep secret the details of the utilities of mass extermination.

² Some of the prisoners and SS-men who had witnessed the atrocities committed at the camp were convinced that the number of murdered victims was as many as several millions. Partially basing their findings eyewitnesses' testimonies, first the Soviet and later the Polish commissions which were appointed in 1945 to examine the crimes that had been perpetrated at the camp came up with a similarly high figure of approximately 4 million. Since the 1950s, however, researchers from various countries have been verifying specific components of this total figure, on the basis of uncovered camp deportation documents, and proving that the original estimates were too high. Most researchers now believe that the number of people killed at Auschwitz was between 1 and 1.5 million, the vast majority of whom (90 percent) were Jews (Franciszek Piper, Auschwitz. How many perished Jews, Poles, Gypsies..., Oświęcim 1996).

³ Josef Mengele, b. 16th March 1911 in Günzburg, Doctor of Philosophy and Medicine. Joined the SS in 1938, where he held various medical posts. Before his arrival at Auschwitz he served as a doctor in the Auxiliary Infantry Battalion *Ost*, which was part of the SS Fifth Armoured Division *Viking*, and saw action on the Eastern Front. After being wounded, he applied to be posted for service in a concentration camp. On 30th May 1943 he began work as a physician at the Gypsy Camp in Auschwitz Birkenau. When the Gypsy camp was closed down in August 1944, Mengele became the chief physician at Birkenau (KL Auschwitz II), and then in November 1944 he also took charge of the camp's SS hospital, a post he held right up to evacuation in Ja-

nuary. During his stay at KL Auschwitz he supervised selections of both newly arrived prisoners on the railway platform as well as of registered inmates. He is most notorious for his experiments carried out on women pregnant with more than one child, on the condition called 'noma' and the heredity of twins and dwarfs. After the war he went into hiding in South America. He drowned in 1979 after suffering a stoke while swimming in the sea not far from Sao Paulo Brazil (Aleksander Lasik, Die Personalbesetzung des Gesundheitsdienstes der SS im Konzentrationslager Auschwitz-Birkenau in den Jahren 1940––1945. In Hefte von Auschwitz 1997 No. 20, p. 314-315; Helena Kubica, Dr. Mengele und seine Verbrechen im Konzentrationslager Auschwitz-Birkenau. in Hefte von Auschwitz 1997 No. 20).

[4] Institute for Racial, Biological and Anthropological Research, which included the Kaiser Wilhelm Institute of Anthropology, Heredity Science and Eugenics (Kaiser Wilhelm Institut für Anthropologie, Menschliche Erblehre und Eugenik), headed by Prof. Otmar von Verschuer – Mengele's mentor and guardian.

[5] After their invasion of Poland in September 1939, Germany and the Soviet Union liquidated the Polish State and occupied its territories. Germany incorporated western Poland into the Reich and created out of central Poland an entity called the General Gouvernement, which had a special legal status. Polish territories were treated as 'living space' (*Lebensraum*) for Germans. Mass deportations and exterminations in places such as concentration camps, ghettos and prisons were carried out for the purpose of removing from occupied territories Poles and other ethnic minorities that had inhabited Poland before the war and replacing them with a German population.

[6] The large-scale transports of Hungarian Jews started arriving at KL Auschwitz in May 1944. As stated in a telegram of the German deputy in Budapest, Edmund Veesenmayer, dated 9 July 1944 – by which time the deportations had practically ceased, following intervention of Regent Miklós Horthy – 437,402 Hungarian Jews were sent to Auschwitz. The first two transports of Hungarian Jews arrived on 2 May. The regular influx of transports began on 16 May. Miklós Nyiszli was on one of these subsequent transports (Randolph L. Braham, *The Destruction of Hungarian Jewry*, New York, 1963, p.443).

[7] The author is referring to Auschwitz concentration camp in Oświęcim and Lublin concentration camp in Lublin, also known as Majdanek.

[8] Auschwitz concentration camp at Oświęcim was opened 14th June 1940 as the first concentration camp in occupied Poland. Within a couple of years it expanded to become the largest Nazi concentration camp in history. Initially Auschwitz comprised the main camp at Oświęcim (from 22nd November 1943 called Auschwitz I). In 1942 new camps were built at Brzezin-

ka/Birkenau (from 22nd November 1943 called Auschwitz II) and Monowice/ Monowitz (which from 22nd November 1943, along with other subsidiary camps, was referred to as Auschwitz III). From 1940 to the spring of 1942 the majority of people deported to Auschwitz and the majority of murdered victims were Poles. The mass deportations of Jews to Auschwitz began in the spring of 1942 as part of the Final Solution programme, which aimed to exterminate Europe's Jewish population of 11 million. Of the 1.3 m people sent to Auschwitz, 1.1 m were Jews, 140-150,000 were Poles, 23,000 were Gypsies, 15,000 were Soviet prisoners-of-war and 2,000 members of various nations, including Byelorussians, Russians, Ukrainians, Czechs, the French, Yugoslavs, Germans and Austrians.

[9] The garrison's chief physician was also in overall charge of the medical service (Department V) at KL Auschwitz, which comprised three sections: general, dental and pharmaceutical. Each section was subdivided into prisoner and SS divisions. The general section was made up of SS doctors looking after the SS personnel and SS doctors dealing with the prisoners – which in reality meant participating in their extermination and producing fictitious death certificates. There were also SS nurses who assisted both categories of SS doctor. The only real chance the inmates had of receiving genuine medical help was from fellow prisoner doctors in the sickbays and so called camp hospitals.

[10] From 1942 Jews deported to Auschwitz underwent selections the moment they got off the train onto the ramp at Auschwitz. The purpose of these selections was to separate those of the newly arrived who were still fit for work from the rest, who were sent straight to the gas chamber. The first gas chamber was built at the main camp in the autumn of 1941. Two more were built at the Birkenau camp in 1942, which were later in 1943, replaced by four modern gas chambers and crematoria. Apart from Jews, several thousand Poles, several thousand Gypsies and several thousand Soviet prisoners-of-war were also killed in the gas chambers.

[11] According to the resolutions of a conference held at Vienna that ended on 6 May 1944, every day four trains were to leave Hungary, taking 3,000 people each. Each train was to be made up of 45 wagons.

[12] The crematoria at Auschwitz were one-storey buildings. The attics of crematoria II and III (I and II) were inhabited by prisoners of the *Sonderkommando* from mid-1944.

[13] There were 4 crematoria at Birkenau. Crematoria II and III (I and II) had just one chimney each, whereas IV and V (III and IV) had two.

[14] The Birkenau camp was divided into building sections (*Bauabschnitte*) – B. Section BI was on the left side of the railway ramp and subdivided into

sections BIa and BIb. BII, to the right of the ramp, was subdivided into seven sections: BIIa, BIIb, BIIc, BIId, BIIf and BIIg. Farther on to right there was also section BIII, which was not completed yet. Some of these sections had their own organisational structures and were officially referred to as camps, thus, for example, section BIIf was known as *Lager* BIIf or the hospital camp.

[15] KL Auschwitz prisoners were marked with numbers. Some 400,000 camp numbers were issued in several series. By far the largest, called the ordinary series – for both men and women – comprised some 300,000 numbers. There was a special series for Gypsy men and women marked with the letter Z, whereas the series for re-educational prisoners had the letters EH and the Russian prisoners-of-war had RKG. Up to 1944, Jewish prisoners were registered in the ordinary series. From May 1944, however, Jewish men and women were registered in a separate series marked A. Once 20,000 series A numbers had been issued, series B numbers were introduced for Jewish men. The A and B letters were tattooed next to the camp number.

[16] According to Third Reich law homosexuality was an offence. Homosexuals had been sent to concentration camps even before the war.

[17] *Lagerführer* (in main camps referred to as *Schutzhaftlagerführer*) – the commander in overall charge of the prisoners in his particular camp section or subsidiary camp. Some parts of the Birkenau camp had their own *Lagerführers* or *Schutzhaftlagerführers* (for example the women's camp, the men's camp and the Gypsies' camp). The posts were usually held by SS officers, or, in the case of some of the smaller subsidiary camps, SS non-commissioned officers. A *Lagerführer* was answerable to the camp commandant or (as was the case in KL Auschwitz III) a *Schutzhaftlagerführer*.

[18] *Leitenderarzt*– the block physician (a prisoner) in overall charge of the block's medical (fellow physicians and nurses) and administrative (block elder and block scribe) personnel.

[19] On the basis of an RSHA (Third Reich Chief Security Office) decree, on 29 January 1943 some 23,000 Gypsies from Germany, the Protectorate in Bohemia and Moravia as wells as other territories directly incorporated into the Reich were arrested and sent to KL Auschwitz. The were interned in a special family camp (BIIe). The camp was set up in February 1943 and closed down in August 1944. A total of approximately 20,000 Gypsies died there.

[20] The football pitch was part of the hospital camp BIIf, situated right next to the unloading ramp and Crematorium II (III). Two numbering systems were used in camp documentation. According to one, Crematorium I was in the Auschwitz main camp, Crematoria II and III were at the end of the unloading ramp at Birkenau, whereas IV and V were situated at the end of the road between camp sections BII and BIII. The other system, used by the author, ig-

181

nores the crematorium in the main camp and numbers the Birkenau crematoria from I to IV.

[21] This was not the case: there was no predetermined schedule for the liquidation of *Sonderkommandos*. 1942 was the only year when whole *Sonderkommandos* were exterminated. Later the prisoners of particular *Sonderkommandos* were killed in batches – by being given phenol injections, tricked into entering chambers where they were then gassed or by various other means. The remaining prisoners were allowed to live in order to maintain a certain continuity in work. Some even managed to survive in the *Sonderkommando* for over two years and, after the war, give evidence on how the gas chambers and crematoria were run (Szlama Dragon and Alter Feinsilber among others).

[22] The number of *Sonderkommando* prisoners was adjusted to the rate of extermination. For example, on 20 April 1944 207 prisoners were employed in all four Birkenau crematoria, whereas on 28 July 1944 there were 873 inmates working in the crematoria, the gas bunker and burning bodies in ditches, not including the 30 prisoners employed to unload the firewood for the ditches.

[23] Erich Muhsfeldt, b. 18 February 1913 in Neubnick Spree. Sentenced to death in Krakow on 22 December 1947. The sentence was carried out.

[24] *Oberkapos* were prisoners in charge of *Kommandos* numbering several hundred people. Below them were the *Kapos*, *Unterkapos* and *Vorarbeiters* (foremen).

[25] According to the German authorities' estimate, the daily output of the four crematoria at Birkenau was 4,416 bodies (crematoria II and III each burned 1440 bodies, whereas IV and V, 768 each). Based on the testimonies of former *Sonderkommando* prisoners, the commission for the study of crimes committed at the camp, headed by Jan Sehn, estimated that the daily output for the four crematoria at Birkenau was 8,000 bodies (2,500 at crematoria II and III and 1,500 at crematoria IV and V).

[26] Reference here should be rather be to functionaries of the *Politische Abteilung*. The commander of the *Politische Abteilung* (Political Department) was simultaneously the representative of the State Police at the camp, in this case the *Staatspolizeileistelle* in Katowice.

[27] See footnote 21.

[28] The author is actually referring to Jews from Poland, Greece, Hungary and France. The *Sonderkommando* was essentially made up of Jews. During Nyszli's time with the *Sonderkommando*, apart from Jews, there was 1 German, 5 Poles and 19 Russian prisoners-of-war.

[29] The *Kleine Postenkette* (small security cordon) comprised guards posted in the watchtowers all along the barbed wire enclosure. The *Grosse Postenkette* (large security cordon) surrounded the camp at a distance of from

several hundred metres to several kilometres. It consisted of watchtowers that were usually occupied by guards over a period from before the time the *Kommandos* marched out to work until after they had returned to the camp. If any prisoners escaped, this outer security cordon was kept continually manned, both day and night, for three days.

[30] This was an improvised gas chamber which was first put into use in the mid 1942, having been converted from a peasant's cottage in the hamlet of Brzezinka. Gassings ceased there with the activation of the four crematoria, but were resumed in May 1944 with the influx of transports of Jews from Hungary. It was initially referred to as the 'White Cottage' or 'Bunker 2', in 1944 it was also referred to as 'Bunker 5'.

[31] Such executions by shooting were rather rare. Most of the corpses burnt in the ditches were of people who had been killed in the gas chamber.

[32] Otto Moll, b. 4th March 1915 in Hochenschönenberg. He served in Auschwitz from May 1941 to January 1945 holding various posts. By the time he was in charge of the crematoria he already had the rank of *Hauptscharführer*. He was tried in proceedings against the staff of Dachau concentration camp, sentenced to death on 13th December 1945, and subsequently executed.

[33] FKL (*Frauenkonzentrationslager*) – women's concentration camp. This ceased being the name of the women's camp at Birkenau on 30 March 1943, when the SS garrison commander shortened it to *Frauenlager*.

[34] The actual figure was 10,000 people. Approximately 3,000 were selected for work and the remaining 7,000 were killed in gas chambers on 11 and 12 July 1944.

[35] Prof. Berthold Epstein MD, a Czech Jew who was in charge of Dr Mengele's laboratory.

[36] For more on the family camp for Jews from the Terezin Ghetto see Miroslav Kárný, 'Das Theresienstädter Familienlager (BIIb) in Birkenau (September 1943-Juli 1944)'. *Hefte von Auschwitz*, 1997, No. 20.

[37] Heinz Thilo, b. in Ebersfeld 8 October 1911. A doctor of medicine. Reached the rank of *Obersturmführer* SS. Served at KL Auschwitz from July 1942 to October 1944 as physician for the SS detachments and camp physician for sections BIIa, BIIc and BIIf. Performed selections among newly arrived Jews on the ramp as well as among prisoners in the camp. Died in Hohenelbe on 13 May 1945.

[38] Concentration camp prisoners received less food than the officially stated 1,300 or 1,700 calories (for those doing hard physical work) a day. A healthy norm for a man doing sedentary work is 2,600 calories and 4,000 calories for one doing hard physical work (*Wielka Encyklopedia Powszechna*, Warsaw 1969, vol. XII, p. 88; Tadeusz Iwaszko, The Housing, Clothing

and Feeding of the Prisoners, in *Auschwitz 1940-1945. Central Issues in the History of the Camp*, Oświęcim 2000, vol. II, p. 59-60).

[39] Reference here is to the village of Rajsko.

[40] Prof., Dr Geza Mansfeld, KL Auschwitz prisoner, instructed by the SS to carry out research into typhus, malaria and syphilis. Liberated at Auschwitz on 27 January 1945, took part in an action to help fellow former prisoners. Later submitted testimonies regarding his imprisonment at the camp and the atrocities committed therein (Danuta Czech, ' Die Rolle des Häftlings-krankenbaulagers im KL Auschwity II' in 1975, No.15).

[41] On 30 June 1944 2,044 Jews arrived at Auschwitz from Athens and Corfu. Out of these, 466 men (camp numbers A 15229 – A 15674) and 175 women (A 8282 – A 8456) were selected for work; the remaining 1,423 were put to death in the gas chambers. Greek Jews were shipped to KL Auschwitz from March 1943 to August 1944 – somewhere between 55 and 65 thousand people in all (Danuta Czech, ' Deportation und Vernichtung der griechischen Juden im KL Auschwitz, im Lichte der sogennanten Endlösung der Judenfrage' in *Hefte von Auschwitz* 1970 No.11; Danuta Czech, *Auschwitz Chronickle 1939–1945.From the Archives of the Auschwitz Memorial and the German Federal Archives,* New York 1997, p. 654).

[42] So far this document has not been recovered. However, six other documents have been found – as a result of searches or by sheer chance: three in 1945, one in 1952, one in 1962 and one in 1980. Four of them had been buried in the vicinity of Crematorium II (III), as referred to by Nyiszli. Five of these six manuscripts have been published in a collection entitled Amidst a Nightmare of Crime. Manuscripts of Members of Sonderkommando, Oświęcim 1973. as well as in *Hefte von Auschwitz* 1973 No.14.

[43] These SS-men are also mentioned in the affidavits and accounts of other *Sonderkommando* members. In documents Seitz and Steinberg appear as SS-*Unterscharführer* Robert Seitz and SS-*Unterscharführer* Karl Fritz Steinberg. There are also photographs of these last two (Aleksander Lasik, *Załoga SS w KL Auschwitz w latach 1940-1945.* Bydgoszcz, 1994).

[44] It was actually called FL (*Frauenlager*) – the women's camp. The women held in this part of the Birkenau camp (sections BIa and BIb) were all registered. The Jewish women who arrived with the Hungarian transports, from May to July 1944, were not registered. The unregistered women selected to work were put in section BIIc, whereas those whom there was not even time to select went to section BIII, which the prisoners called 'Mexico'. The latter camp section was not yet completed and often the women prisoners had to sleep out in the open air. Nor were they provided with adequate clothing. Selections were eventually carried out in both camp sections, after which some

of the women were sent to work in other parts of the camp, to subsidiary camps or to altogether different camps while others were sent to the gas chamber.

[45] It actually happened on the 7th.

[46] According to documentation, there were actually 663 people employed in the *Sonderkommando* on 7 October 1944.

[47] Ala Gertner, Regina Szafirsztajn and Estera Wajcblum. The explosives were smuggled in by Róża Robota, who worked in the *Effektenlager* close to Crematorium III (IV). All these women were later investigated and subsequently hanged on 6 January 1945 in a new part of the Auschwitz main camp called the *Schutzhaftlagererweiterung*.

[48] Other sources do not mention any firearms in *Sonderkommando's* possession apart from some crude, home-made grenades

[49] The revolt broke out when the SS tried to take another 300 prisoners away from the *Sonderkommando*. During it prisoners set fire to bunks in the undressing room of Crematorium III(IV), where most of the *Sonderkommando* employed at Crematorium IV(V) and the 'gas bunker' were quartered.

[50] The *Sonderkommando* was supposed to take part in a planned revolt that encompassed the whole camp and was co-ordinated with an attack by partisan detachments. The SS attempt to liquidate the *Sonderkommando* forced its prisoners to rebel before the planned time. Only the prisoners of Crematorium I (II) joined in the revolt of Crematorium III (IV).

[51] No other source confirms Nyiszli's figures regarding SS losses. According SS garrison order No. 26/44 on 7 October 1944 three SS-men 'died fighting the enemy, faithfully upholding their oath to the Führer': Rudolf Erler, Willi Freese and Jozef Purke. According to a former Sonderkommando prisoner, twelve SS-men were wounded. Prisoner losses included 451 dead. 212 *Sonderkommando* prisoners survived, mainly the ones from crematoria IV(V) and II(III), who did not participate in the revolt.

[52] Should be 7 October 1944.

[53] The Łódź Ghetto was set up on 8 February 1940. Apart from the Jews of Łódź, it held Jews from the so-called *Wartheland*, Germany and other countries. In all, at one time or another there were some 260,000 Jews in the ghetto. The physically fit were made to work in local industrial plants, those who were unable to work were shipped out to extermination camps. The ghetto was liquidated in August 1944. The 60-70,000 surviving Jews were shipped to KL Auschwitz, where on arrival most were immediately sent to the gas chambers.

[54] Terezin – a fortress and garrison town built in the 18th century, situated several dozen kilometres to the north of Prague. In November 1941 the Germans set up a central ghetto for Czech Jews there, though they also brought

in Jews from Germany, Austria and other countries. Of the 140,000 Jewish inhabitants, 34,000 died in the ghetto and a further 83,000 were sent to various extermination camps, including 46,000 who were sent to Auschwitz.

[55] The order to cease all mass exterminations in the gas chambers must have been issued earlier because a transport of Jews from Sered in Slovakia that arrived at Auschwitz on 3 November did not undergo a selection, instead all the Jews were taken to the camp and registered. The dismantling of crematoria I(II) and II(III) began on 25 November.

[56] The *Sonderkommando* comprised 200 men at the time.

[57] The SS probably tried but failed to burn properly on one of the pyres the bodies of another 100 *Sonderkommando* prisoners who had been shot. They then took the remains to Crematorium IV (V), which was the only crematorium working at time.

[58] Should be 7.

[59] Fritz Klein, b. 24 November 1888 in Zeiden. A medical doctor. At KL Auschwitz from December 1943 to January 1945. Rose to the rank of SS-*Obersturmführer*. Condemned to death in the trial of Bergen-Belsen staff and executed on 13 December 1945.

[60] Both groups were sentenced to death by a court martial made up of Gestapo officials from Katowice.

[61] This was not the case. In fact Auschwitz was officially a 'concentration camp', that is, *Konzentrationslager*, to the end of its existence. The term 'labour camp' was applied to KL Auschwitz subsidiary camps, though they were actually an integral part of the whole concentration camp complex.

[62] The crematoria were actually right next to the camp. Nyiszli is most probably referring to the camp's main gate.

[63] During their flight from the camp, the SS set fire to 30 barracks where the victims' looted belongings were sorted and stored. These warehouses were located in section BIIg between crematoria II (III) and III (IV).

[64] Apart from the above mentioned complex of 30 barracks, the SS also blew up the crematoria and gas chambers, but no other buildings were destroyed. On the other hand, documents were burnt throughout the camp in order to erase incriminating evidence. Despite this, some camp records did survive.

[65] On 17 January 1945 there were still 67,012 prisoners, men, women and children, in the various Auschwitz camps and subsidiary camps. This figure included 4,473 prisoners from the men's camp at Birkenau. Like the others, on 18 January they set out in several columns bound for Wodzisław Śląski, which is 63 km from the Birkenau site. The camp was liberated by Soviet troops on 27 January 1945.

[66] This fact is confirmed in the accounts of other prisoners. The incident occurred before a bridge over the Vistula at a place called Góra. However, other accounts only mention shots being fired over the column of prisoners. The SS were most probably fighting partisans, because the Russians were still in Krakow on 18 January 1945.

INDEX OF NAMES

GEOGRAPHICAL INDEX

CONTENTS

1. 2. Birkenau 1944. Jewish transports from Hungary. '...*four or five transports of deportees were arriving from Hungary every day.*' Photo by SS, 1944.

3. 4. Birkenau. The unloading ramp. In the top left and right corners one can see the buildings of crematoria I (II) and II (III). Photo by SS, 1944.

5. 6. '*I observed from afar; the elegant cloths, trench coats and fashionable bags told me that they were probably from one of the major cities.*'
Photo by SS, 1944.

7. 8. '*Men, women and children were made to walk past the commission in single file. With a hand gesture from the selecting physician, ... some went to the left, others to the right.*' Photo by SS, 1944.

9. 10. *'The newcomers slowly approached the camp in long columns, in fives, flanked by the SS.'* Photo by SS, 1944.

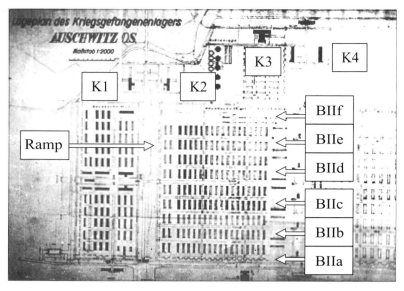

11. Map of the Birkenau. The four crematoria and gas chambers (K1 – K4) are shown at the top.

12. Allied aerial photograph of the Birkenau camp showing gas chambers and crematoria (II and III).

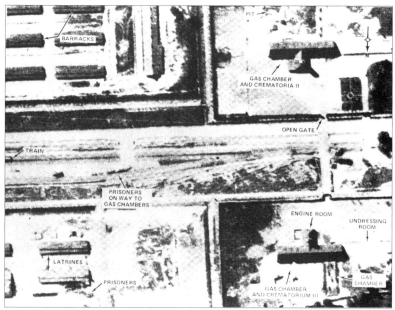

13. Crematorium I (II) still being built '...*the redbrick building with its chimney throwing out flames. This was the premises of one of the crematoria.*' Photo by SS, 1943.

14. Crematorium III (IV) at Birkenau, later burnt down during the revolt of the *Sonderkommando* on 7th October 1944. Photo by SS, 1943.

15. Crematorium I (II). '...fifteen fiery ovens. The corpses of the old, the young and children lay in a long row on the concrete floor.' Photo by SS, 1943.
16. Map of Crematorium I (II).

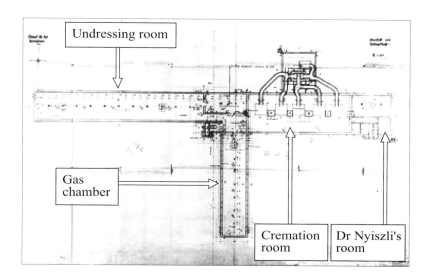

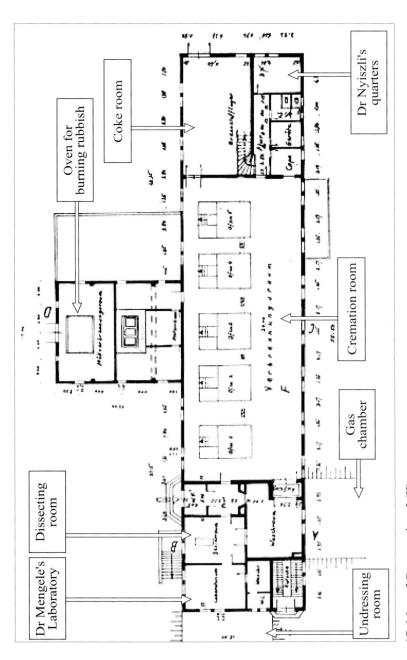

Dr Mengele's Laboratory

Dissecting room

Oven for burning rubbish

Coke room

Dr Nyiszli's quarters

Cremation room

Gas chamber

Undressing room

17. Map of Crematorium I (II)

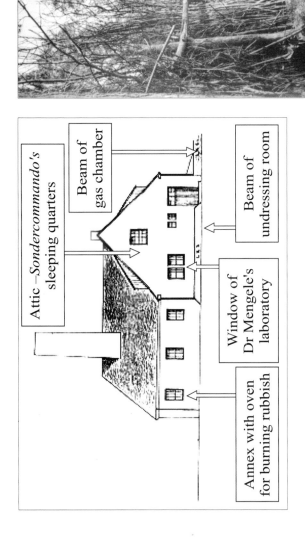

18. Map of Crematorium I (II). West-facing side.
19. A fence made of branches concealing crematoria and gas chambers. Photo by Stanisław Kołowca, 1945.

Attic –*Sondercommando's* sleeping quarters

Beam of gas chamber

Beam of undressing room

Window of Dr Mengele's laboratory

Annex with oven for burning rubbish

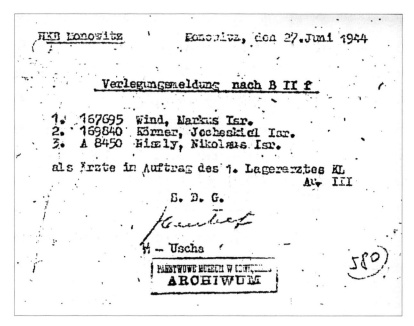

20. Command dated 27th June 1944 for the transfer of three prisoners from the Monowitz camp to Birkenau, including Miklós Nyiszli (Nikolaus Niszly).
21. Fragment of a work report, dated 3rd October 1944, stating the number of *Sonderkommando* prisoners (*Heizer*) employed at each crematorium all together 661 helpers and 3 experts.

Kdo.Nr.	Arbeitskommandos.					
	Übertrag:		63		1621 5521	
	Dienststellen - Verwaltung:					
51-B.	Baubetriebsdienststellen	Lager	-	52	65	52 65
52-B.	Aufräumungskdo. Au. I.	Ausch.	-	-	5o	
53-B.	Aufräumungskdo. Au. II. N. Entw.	Lager	-	-	472	
54-B.	Aufräumungskdo. Au. II. a.d. R.	Lager	-	-	280	- 802
57-B.	Heizer Krematorium I. Tag	Lager	1	2	84	
57-B.	Heizer Krematorium I. Nacht	Lager	2	-	85	
58-B.	Heizer Krematorium II. Nacht	Lager	2	-	85	
58-B.	Heizer Krematorium II. Tag	Lager	1	-	84	
59-B.	Heizer Krematorium III. Tag	Lager	1	1	84	
59-B.	Heizer Krematorium III. Nacht	Lager	2	-	85	
6o-B.	Heizer Krematorium IV. Nacht	Lager	2	-	84	
6o-B.	Heizer Krematorium IV. Tag	Lager	1	-	7o	3 661
			12		55 1529	
	Läuferposten	Lagerber. 2				
	Gesamt:		77		1676 6911	

B II/a. B II/d. B II/e. B II/f. 3 II/g.
H. 20 1110 450 55 61

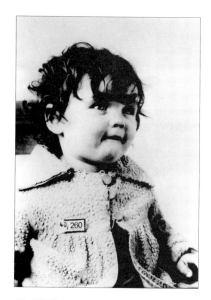

22. Siblings Johannes and Erdmann Schmidt both these Gypsy children were experimented on by Dr Mengele and subsequently died at Auschwitz.

Hyg.-bakt. Unters.-Stelle
der Waffen-SS, Südost

29. JUN. 1944

Auschwitz OS., am 29. Juni 1944.

Anliegend wird übersandt:
(12-jähriges Kind)
Material: **Kopf einer Leiche** entnommen am
zu untersuchen auf **Histologische Schnitte**

Name, Vorname:
Dienstgrad, Einheit: **siehe Anlage**
Klinische Diagnose:

Anschrift der einsendenden Dienststelle: **H.-Krankenbau**
Zigeunerlager Auschwitz II, B II e

Bemerkungen:
Der 1. Lagerarzt
K.L. Auschwitz II

SS-Hauptsturmführer.
(Stempel, Unterschrift)

23. Note sent by Dr Mengele to the Institute of Hygiene at Rajsko for the carrying out of a histopathological study on the severed head of a twelve- -year-old girl.

24. SS Hauptsturmführer Josef Mengele. *'Because general autopsies and examinations of particular organs had to be carried out simultaneously, the twins in the experimental barracks of section BIId died simultaneously Doctor Mengele killed them... This same criminal would spend hours sittii beside me among the microscopes, test tubes and flasks or standing at the dissecting table in a bloodstained apron examining and rummaging with bloodstained hands. All for the sake of increasing the procreation of the Germanic race...'*

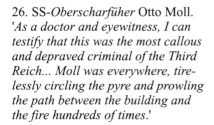

25. SS-*Oberscharführer* Erich Muhsfeld(t). *'It is of no concern to me if I shoot eighty or a thousand people.'*

26. SS-*Oberscharführer* Otto Moll. *'As a doctor and eyewitness, I can testify that this was the most callous and depraved criminal of the Third Reich... Moll was everywhere, tirelessly circling the pyre and prowling the path between the building and the fire hundreds of times.'*

27. Prisoners of the Sonderkommando burning bodies in the open air close to Crematorium IV (V). Photograph secretly taken by a Greek Jewish prisoner called Alexis in 1944.

29. Alter Feinsilber (Stanisław Jankowski, 1910 – 1987), employed in the *Sonderkommando* from 1942 to 1945. He escaped during the evacuation of Auschwitz and settled in Paris after the war. Seen here at the site of Auschwitz I in 1985. Photo by Lidia Foryciarz.

28. Jankiel Handelsman. One of the leaders of the *Sonderkommando* revolt. '*...with guns constantly blazing, the SS-men proceeded to storm the entrance to Crematorium III (IV).*'